Power Struggle

Cycle B Sermons for Proper 18 Through
Reign of Christ
Based On The Gospel Lessons

Wayne Brouwer

CSS Publishing Company
Lima, Ohio

POWER STRUGGLE

FIRST EDITION
Copyright © 2023
by CSS Publishing Co., Inc.

Library of Congress Cataloging-in-Publication Data:

Names: Brouwer, Wayne, 1954- author.
Title: Power struggle : Cycle B sermons for proper 18 through reign of
  Christ based on the gospel lessons / Wayne Brouwer.
Description: First edition. | Lima, Ohio : CSS Publishing Company, Inc.,
  [2023]
Identifiers: LCCN 2023028741 (print) | LCCN 2023028742 (ebook) | ISBN
  9780788030888 (paperback) | ISBN 9780788030895 (adobe pdf)
Subjects: LCSH: Bible. Mark--Sermons. | Bible. Mark--Criticism,
  interpretation, etc.
Classification: LCC BS2585.54 .B76 2023 (print) | LCC BS2585.54 (ebook) |
  DDC 226.3/06--dc23/eng/20230814
LC record available at https://lccn.loc.gov/2023028741
LC ebook record available at https://lccn.loc.gov/2023028742

For more information about CSS Publishing Company resources, visit our website at www.csspub.com, email us at csr@csspub.com, or call (800) 241-4056.

e-book:
ISBN-13: 978-0-7880-3089-5
ISBN-10: 0-7880-3089-2

ISBN-13: 978-0-7880-3088-8
ISBN-10: 0-7880-3088-4   PRINTED IN USA

Contents

Introduction: Good News Through Mark 5

Proper 17 / Ordinary Time 22 ....Mark 7:1-8, 14-15, 21-23
Inside Out.. 15

Proper 18 / Ordinary Time 23 .... Mark 7: 24-37
The Price Of Popularity 23

Proper 19 / Ordinary Time 24 .... Mark 8:27-38
Mistaken Identity.. 30

Proper 20 / Ordinary Time 25 .... Mark 9:30-37
Majoring In Minors 38

Proper 21 / Ordinary Time 26 .... Mark 9:38-50
Heaven's Culture 48

Proper 22 / Ordinary Time 27 .... Mark 10:2-16
Bonding And Confidence 57

Proper 23 / Ordinary Time 28 .... Mark 10:17-31
Inverted Reality 66

Proper 24 / Ordinary Time 29 .... Mark 10:35-45
Up The Ladder To Nowhere 75

Proper 25 / Ordinary Time 30 .... Mark 10:46-52
"I Want to See" 81

Proper 26 / Ordinary Time 31 .... Mark 12:28-34
Navigation Assist 85

Proper 27 / Ordinary Time 32 .... Mark 12:38-44
Public Piety? 91

Proper 28 / Ordinary Time 33 .... Mark 13:1-8
Chaos...101

Reign of Christ – Proper 29 / Ordinary Time 34 .... John 18:33-37
King Jesus 106

Introduction: Good News Through Mark

Although the gospels of the New Testament are among the most widely recognized and read documents in the world, it remains difficult to explain their exact genre. The gospels have no clear parallel in any other religious or literary tradition.

A Unique Form Of Writing

Certainly, the gospels are not mere biographies. They do not offer enough data about the life of Jesus to construct a full story of his existence, or to offer a well-developed social portrait of his presence among his contemporaries. While Matthew (1:18-2:23) and Luke (1:5-2:40) each related a few events surrounding Jesus' birth, their selections differ significantly from one another. Luke briefly told of a single incident in Jesus' early adolescence (2:41-52), and then jumped quickly to Jesus' baptism by John, indicating that this took place when Jesus "was about thirty years old" (2:23). The bulk of all four gospels proceed from this inaugurating event, bypassing almost entirely Jesus' first three decades of life. Since John included notes about Jesus participating in three Passover celebrations (2:13-25; 6:4; 13:1), the last of which became the occasion for his crucifixion, it is commonly assumed that Jesus was thirty-three years old when he died. But the gospels are certainly not clear, concise, or comprehensive biographies of Jesus' life.

Nor is it true that the gospels are a complete and systematic summary of Jesus' teachings. What has been preserved as the record of Jesus' sayings and speeches is too haphazardly gathered to form a codified compendium that would neatly explain his wisdom or theology. Indeed, while Jesus' parables, sermons, and dialogues are essential to the gospels, the activities of Jesus' life also remain important, even though they do not form a detailed biographical life history. One significant example of this is the Passion narrative, found in all four gospels. There is a deliberate and extensive accounting of what happened during Jesus' last week in Jerusalem, to the extent that approximately one-third of each gospel is consumed by this brief and critical event. If the gospels were intended primarily as teachings of the master, they would not likely give so much place to these other dimensions of Jesus' life.

The most fitting designation for the gospels seems to be that of "proclamation." These documents are records of early Christian preaching about Jesus, describing the significance of his coming, the meaning of his personhood, the content of his teachings, the importance of his actions, the character of his death, and the miracle of his resurrection. Moreover, all of this material is communicated as a means to espouse a particular understanding of the divine mind and initiatives among the human race. The gospels are the church's early homilies.

Although the designations that give name to each of the four canonical gospels are extremely familiar ("The gospel according to Matthew," "...Mark," "...Luke," "...John"), these were added by the early church on the basis of traditions which emerged very early in the transcription process. Apart from the brief introduction in Luke's gospel (1:1-4), and the few words of personal reflection at the end of chapters 20 and 21 of John's gospel, those who originally penned these documents had no desire to claim the contents for themselves, nor call attention to their own part in the activities recounted. The purpose of these writings was to proclaim Jesus, and that they did.

The Arrival Of The "Day Of The Lord" Through Peter's/Mark's Voice
The ascription of authorship tied each of the gospels to a particular provenance and purpose early in its existence, and this is important for those who try to probe the uniqueness of each document. Although New Testament scholars continue to debate whether these presumed writers actually penned the proclamations attributed to them, no widely affirmed, viable alternatives have ever been put forward. So, the Gospel according to Mark is as well interpreted as any through the eyes of Papias, a second century bishop, who declared (according to Eusebius in Book 33 of his *Church History*): "Mark, who was Peter's interpreter, wrote down accurately, though not in order, all that he remembered of what Christ had said or done."

Who Was Mark?

What do we know of this Mark about whom Papias wrote? Most of our data comes from the book of Acts in the New Testament, along with snippets from the "greetings" sections of Paul's and Peter's letters. The man had at least two names (Acts 12:12; 12:25; 15:37), which was not unusual in his world: *John* was probably used mostly in his Palestinian Jewish context, and *Mark* provided a Hellenized name for interaction with the larger Roman world. From the twelfth chapter of Acts we glean a few interesting tidbits about Mark's early life, growing up in Jerusalem. He is called the "son of Mary," probably indicating that there had been no husband/father in the household for some time. Most likely this meant that Mark's father had died while he was still relatively young.

Furthermore, it is clear from the same passage that Mary's house was the meeting place for the early Jerusalem Christian congregation. When Peter was imprisoned, the Christ-believers of the city gathered for an all-night prayer meeting at this location. Indeed, Peter himself was aware of it, so that when he came to his senses after his middle-of-the-night miraculous release, although he was not a native of the place, he quickly found his way to Mary's home, expecting help.

The description of the house itself also indicated that Mary was a woman who lived in the more well-to-do part of Jerusalem. When Peter arrived at her home, he knocked for entrance on a gate that was separated from the living quarters by a courtyard. This arrangement was only true for those with some financial means, and was not common for most people whose domestic space abutted the street. Evidently John Mark was from the wealthier part of town.

This information supports a strong probable connection between Mark and the priestly ruling class within first century Palestinian Judaism. Mark's tribal background, after all, was Levite. His cousin Barnabas (Colossians 4:10), was a wealthy Levite who had a second home on the island of Cyprus (Acts 4:36). It was probably because of this family link that Mark traveled with Barnabas and Paul to become part of the first Christian church planted outside of Palestine, in the old Greek administrative city of Antioch (Acts 11:27—30; 12:25), and then joined the pair on their initial mission journey into Asia Minor (Acts 13:1—5). Something happened during those travels, which caused Mark to return home to Jerusalem (Acts 14:36) before the rest. Different speculations suggest that Mark might have been angered at the changing role between Barnabas and Paul,[1] or that the harsh experiences of the journey proved too much for Mark to endure. In any case, his failure to go the distance later caused a difficult rift between Barnabas and Paul, to the extent that they parted in anger (Acts 15:38—42).

Mark and Paul were eventually reconciled, as made clear when, a decade later, Paul would write that Mark was his faithful fellow worker (Colossians 4:10; Philemon 24). Near the end of Paul's life, he even called Mark a useful assistant whom Paul wanted to have with him as he faced martyrdom (2 Timothy 4:11). Peter also, just a few years earlier, had called Mark "my son" (2 Peter 5:13), indicating the close bond that had developed between Mark and the key leaders of the apostolic church.

Some rather strange and interesting glimpses of Mark have filtered through the pages of scripture and history. First, only in the gospel attributed to Mark does this very unusual note about someone who observed Jesus' arrest appear: "A young man, wearing nothing but a linen garment, was following Jesus. When they seized him he fled naked, leaving his garment behind" (Mark 14:51—52). Since this incident seems to add nothing to the theology of the gospel, it is often thought that here Mark made a single reference to his own experiences, growing up in Jerusalem during the years of controversy swirling about Jesus.

Second, there are several references to a nickname gained by Mark in the early church. Transliterated from Greek, the appellation would be *"Kolobodaktulos,"* a word that meant "stubby finger."[2] One story suggests that Mark gained this name because he was born into the home of a priest's family. At the age of 25 he should have become an apprentice priest in the temple, along with all other unblemished males from priestly families. But by this time Mark had become a follower of Jesus, and no longer believed it would be proper to continue offering animal sacrifices. In order to mar his features physically, so that he would become disqualified from priestly duty, he cut off part of one of his fingers. Although this report cannot be confirmed, it is interesting to note that when Paul and Barnabas take young John Mark with them on their first mission journey, he is called an "assistant," using the same Greek term which also designated the apprentice priests in the temple.

---

1   It seemed that Barnabas' younger protégé was actually becoming the leader of the group, since in his reporting of their travels it was always "Barnabas and Paul" until they had finished crossing Cyprus, after which the two were listed as "Paul and Barnabas"

2   cf. Hippolytus, *Philosophumena*, VII, xxx.

What Was Mark Trying To Communicate?

Papias knew that the church of his day recognized this shortest of the gospels as consisting essentially of the preaching of Peter about Jesus, even though the words themselves were recorded by Mark. There are several internal hints to support this hypothesis: Peter's call to be a follower of Jesus is the first to be recorded (Mark 1:16), even though each of the gospels reports the various callings in different sequences; Peter is identified as "Simon" early in the gospel (Mark 1:16, 29, 36), which fits with the probable way Peter was addressed by his family and friends, before Jesus renamed him (Mark 3:16) "Rocky" (the essential meaning of the Greek name "Peter"); the story of Jesus healing Peter's mother-in-law is told with more personal detail (Mark 1:29—37) than is found in its other gospel recordings (Matthew 8:14—15; Luke 4:38—39). Together these clues cement a close connection between Mark's gospel and the preaching of Peter. Like as not, the old apostle declared these remembrances to his congregation in Rome, and his younger assistant took down notes that eventually morphed into this earliest gospel.

The first glimpse of Jesus in the gospel according to Mark was found immediately in the introductory heading or title of 1:1— "The beginning of the good news (gospel) about Jesus Christ, the Son of God." Several things are important in this short statement. First, the author presumed there was much more to declare about Jesus than that which would be contained in these proclamations; this is only "the beginning." Second, whatever one might think about Jesus, even with the gruesome crucifixion story still ahead, the impact of his life and ministry is "good news." This colors how one should receive the message that followed. Third, Jesus was already understood at the beginning of this story to be the Messiah foretold by the prophets of the Old Testament. The term "Christ," appended to "Jesus," was a title, not a name (although it would come to be used as such). Jesus was "the Christ," meaning the one anointed to be the great deliverer of the Jews. This is why the baptism and divine commissioning of Jesus are told first (Mark 1:9—11), and are clearly expressed as a divine anointing (verse 10). Fourth, an additional designation is given to Jesus; he is called "the Son of God." While Christianity has made this a common theological phrase, it was originally a very specific political term used to honor the Roman emperor. When Caesar Augustus died, the Roman Senate declared him to be divine. All of the rulers who came after him were, in turn, identified as the "Son of God," when they mounted the throne. For Mark to call Jesus the "Son of God" was a deliberate move to identify him as a rival to the Roman emperor of the day.

Our initial impressions about Jesus, as the narrative unfolds, are those showing him to be a man of action, healing and power. In the first two chapters alone, Jesus was breathlessly busy, flitting all over Galilee, healing and teaching with such abandon that he is constantly followed (Mark 1:45), and always under urgent demand (Mark 3:7—8). While the gospel seems, at the start, to be merely a collection of stories about Jesus' healings and brief teachings, it soon begins to take linear shape. In fact, its literary form will be copied by Matthew and Luke, who depend extensively on Mark's record. This is why these three are together called the synoptics (those who see similarly). In very broad outline the gospel of Mark looks like this:

> **Chapters 1-8** Jesus blasts the powers that harm human life by means of the greater power of the kingdom of God
> *Transitional Event*: Transfiguration in chapter 9

> **Chapters 9-10** Jesus teaches his close companions about the cost and character of discipleship
> *Transitional Event*: Entry into Jerusalem in chapter 11

> **Chapters 11-16** Jesus moves to the cross and beyond in a fulfillment of the cost of discipleship upon himself, and a paradoxical expression of the power of the kingdom of God

How Did Mark's Message Flow?

Among the many things that can be said about Mark's gospel, there are a number of interesting and critical features that are unique to it. First, no infancy story is recorded (in distinction from Matthew and Luke). This gospel about Jesus begins with his full-grown adult powers in place, and these are immediately confirmed and amplified by the commissioning endowment of the divine Spirit. In other words, according to Peter's preaching and Mark's penning, Jesus jumps out of the starting gate at full throttle, a man on a mission, with energy and purpose.

Second, the prophecy of Isaiah is recalled up front. That Old Testament spokesperson announced the coming of the great Day of the

Lord, speaking of a time when Yahweh would break into human history to bring judgment against the nations of the world and the evil in Israel, save a remnant, and begin the new and transforming messianic age. In this way, Mark linked the coming of Jesus directly to the Old Testament identity of God, and the actions of salvation history contained in it, including the "Day of the Lord" expectations. This connection was further affirmed when Jesus opened his mouth to preach. His very first words were written by Mark as "the good news of God" (1:14), and commence as a staccato summary of the prophetic "Day of the Lord" theology: "The time has come. The kingdom of God is near. Repent and believe the good news!" (1:15).

Third, within the body of Mark's gospel, Jesus' first extended teaching was the parable of the Sower and Seeds (Mark 4:1—20). Its placing and expansive size, in comparison to the snippets of teaching that came earlier, highlight it as distinctive and important. As one reads these pages in continuous narrative, the pace suddenly slows, and Jesus demanded that we reflect on what had happened so far. We had been watching the Jesus of power and action through the eyes of Peter and Mark. Now we must respond to the person of Jesus. How will the sower's seed find perch in our own lives? What kind of soil are we? Both for Jesus' initial audience and for those who encounter Jesus through this gospel, the multiple-layered metaphor serves as a call to self-assessment and belief. Reaching behind the literary origins of the gospel, it is clear to see that Peter was not preaching merely to communicate information, nor was Mark recording Peter's sermons as a nice collection of spiritual writings. This was a document intended for volitional reaction. One *must* respond to Jesus, and the outcome of that engagement would be seen in direct changes of lifestyle and behavior.

Fourth, the healings (particularly the raising of the dead girl) in chapter 5, appear to trigger public animosity which will eventually lead to Jesus' death. Chapter 6 opened with the first major negative reaction against Jesus; it was predicated on the idea that people like the "magic tricks" of Jesus' miracles, but they didn't appreciate having a local boy regarded as messianically special. What was received as "good news" by the crowds became bad news for the social and religious leaders. Without credentials, this man was challenging their authority, since the presence and power of God seemed to flow much more easily and immediately than it did through them.

Fifth, this divided outlook about Jesus' actions and character may well be the reason for the unique and somewhat odd emphasis in Mark's gospel toward what has come to be known as the "Messianic Secret." On a number of occasions, when Jesus healed someone, he gave orders for the miracle to be kept quiet (Mark 1:34; 1:43—44; 3:12; 5:43; 8:26; 8:30; 9:9). While there are a few instances in which Jesus encouraged people to talk about what he had done (such as Mark 5:18—20), it seemed that most of the time Jesus did not want his mighty works widely publicized. Although it may seem contradictory for Jesus to expend the energy of heaven so dramatically and then wrap it up in a blanket of secrecy, there was probably good reason for the hushing. Crowds, titillated by these unusual events, might have quickly developed into mobs that could have short-circuited his full messianic task by trying to crown him as king too early, and only in a temporal realm (see Mark 1:45). If that had happened, Jesus could have ended up becoming merely a temporary human teacher, bogged down with the care of an endless stream of clients looking for a quick fix to their perceived problems. For that reason, Mark recorded Jesus' urgent warnings, early in his career, for people not to tell what has happened. Later, as the crisis of his life and identity heated up, these warnings were no longer necessary.

Sixth, while all the evangelists reported Jesus' entry into Jerusalem at the time of his final Passover in very similar manners, each nuanced the details in a way that hinted at the larger themes intended through their writings. In the case of Mark, there was an immediate shadow of rejection reported in the events of the day. "Jesus entered Jerusalem and went to the temple," wrote Mark in 11:11. But then he added this peculiar assessment: "He looked around at everything, but since it was already late, he went out to Bethany with the twelve."

While it is certainly possible to take this statement as a mere reference to the lengthened shadow on the sundial, Mark coupled it immediately with the cleansing of the temple and the cursing of the fig tree. Each of these actions was an overt judgment of Jesus imputed on the religious system of the day. The first rails against the leaders, who have allowed the temple ceremonies to become something foreign from their original purposes, while the latter castigated the nation as a whole for not fulfilling its Sinai covenant mission. The image of the fig tree (or similar domesticated flora) was a recognized cipher in the

Old Testament, used to refer to Israel as the unique partner with Yahweh for the blessing of the nations (see Psalm 80; Isaiah 5:1—7; Micah 7:1—6; Jeremiah 8:13). Although it may not have been the season of the annual cycle for this particular tree to bear figs, there was never a time when the planting of Yahweh was not to produce fruits as evidence of its unique mission in the divine global recovery plan. When Jesus cursed the tree, even though it was not the season for it to hang with ripe figs, he was using it as a metaphor or teaching tool for those who heard him.

Mark assured us that this was Jesus' meaning when cursing the tree, for he added Jesus' teaching that through true belief "this mountain" (the place where Jerusalem and the temple were built) could be tossed into the sea. In other words, there was a shift in the mission methods of God taking place through Jesus' ministry. This city and nation, which had been the political, temporal, and geographical vehicle for announcing Yahweh's presence to the world, were now relinquishing those ties. In its wake would come a new focus on the person and work of Jesus, portable in its delivery to all nations through the preaching of his followers.

What Is The Impact?

This message is confirmed at the close of the gospel. The last person to make a declaration about Jesus in Mark's version of the gospel proclamation is the centurion at the cross (Mark 15:38—39). As the overwhelming impact of Jesus' crucifixion began to shudder through the world, this soldier made a powerful and overtly religious/political testimony. When he entered the ranks of the Roman military he had had to take an oath of loyalty to the emperor, the "son of god." Here at Jesus' cross, however, he began to understand that there was a ruler above the man in Rome. Although this person was dying in the ignominy of a social reject, there was something about him that announced a grander outlook on life, and called for a bigger allegiance in order to make sense of his brief existence. The centurion, in a dramatic transferal of his military oath, publicly declared, "Surely *this* man was the Son of God!"

As a message first being preached by Peter in Rome during the days when Nero was coming to power, and then read by the Christians of Rome while official persecutions were mounted against them, the implication of the "good news" about Jesus was incredibly political.

Nero demanded obedience through force; yet even his own soldiers recognized that in Jesus was a higher power, a greater power, a more worthy power that alone could overcome all of the other powers which enslaved people through demon possession, dehumanization, disease, or even death.

Taken as a whole, the "good news" about the "Son of God" in Mark's gospel is clear. Jesus is the heaven-sent Christ (Messiah or "anointed one") who arrived as the means by which the "Day of the Lord" would be accomplished in both judgment and blessing. Jesus tore into his world with action and power, overturning the many threats to human existence, and bringing the healing graces of restoration and hope. Because people might misinterpret his miracles and want to make him their trophy ruler too quickly, Jesus cautioned recipients of his transforming power to keep quiet about those things. Finally, when the big confrontation between Jesus and those who seemed to hold social authority is unavoidable, Jesus declares a new strategy in the divine redemptive mission that takes the old "promised land" out of the picture, commissions his close followers begin a "good news" blitz to the nations, and changes all the rules of the game by dying in pain and shame in order to be reborn in power and hope.

Inside Out

Fred Craddock told of a vacation encounter in the Smokey Mountains of eastern Tennessee years ago that moved him deeply. He and his wife took supper one evening in a place called the Black Bear Inn. One side of the building was all glass, open to a magnificent mountain view. Glad to be alone, the Craddocks were a bit annoyed when an elderly man ambled over and struck up a nosy conversation: "Are you on vacation?" "Where are you from?" "What do you do?"

When he discovered that Fred taught in a seminary, the man suddenly had a preacher story to tell. "I was born back here in these mountains," he said. "My mother was not married, and her shame fell upon me. The children at school called me horrible names. During recess I would go hide in the weeds until the bell rang," he told Fred. "At lunchtime I took my lunch and went behind a tree to avoid them.

"Things got worse when I went to town. Men and women would stare at my mother and me, trying to guess the identity of my father. About seventh or eighth grade, I started to go hear a preacher. He wore a claw hammer tailcoat, striped trousers, and had a face that looked like it had been quarried out of the mountain. He frightened me in a way, and he attracted me in a way. His voice thundered.

"I was afraid of what people would say to me, so I'd sneak into church just in time for the sermon, then rush out quickly when it was done. One Sunday, some women had cued up in the aisle and I couldn't get out and I began to get cold and sweaty and was sure that somebody would challenge me, `What's a boy like you doing in church?'

"Suddenly I felt a hand on my shoulder. I looked out of the corner of my eye and saw that beard and saw that face. The minister stared at me and I thought, 'Oh, no. Oh, no. He's gonna guess.'

"The minister focused a penetrating glare at me and then said, `Well boy, you're a child of ah . . . You're a child of ah . . . Ah, wait.' The preacher paused dramatically, getting ready to announce the horrible revelation to the church. Then he said, `You're a child of God! I see a strikin' resemblance!'

"He swatted me on the bottom," said the old man, "and then told me, 'Go claim your inheritance, boy!'"

Fred Craddock looked more closely at the old man and asked, "What's your name?"

As the gentleman got up to wander on, he proudly replied, "Ben Hooper!" Fred remembered his own father telling him about the time when for two terms the people of Tennessee had elected an illegitimate governor named Ben Hooper. The outcast had survived. The shamed had succeeded. The boy of infamy was transformed into a man of fame and stature.

How does it happen? How does shame turn to self-assurance and guilt to grace? How did Ben Hooper, a child of social poverty, emerge as a leader of society?

Erik Erikson, the social analyst, said it happens when greatness finds itself. In fact, Erikson used that theme to describe the early years of another "nobody" who vaulted to world fame, the great reformer Martin Luther. Erikson reflected on what it was that made Luther a man who could change world history; his assessment was that in Luther, greatness found itself. Luther, he said, was someone who had the seeds of greatness within him, and through the circumstances of his life, he eventually found what it took to make a difference.

In can happen to anyone, said Dr. Erikson. Usually, however, the transition from ordinary existence to greatness happens when people are forced to endure three major crises of life and manage to face themselves honestly each time.

Identity Crisis

The first is the identity crisis. It's the crisis we face when we ask ourselves who we really are — not just what this job has made us. It is not just what Mom and Dad think we should be and not just the roles we play with our friends, but who we really are. It is what makes us special, different, and unique among the billions of other bodies occupying space on planet earth.

Tony Campolo once told of a student who came to him in his office at Eastern Christian College. The young man explained to Dr. Campolo that he was going to take a semester off from college in order to travel for a while and get away from all the pressures that were consuming him. He said, "I don't know who I am anymore." Because of the expectations laid on him by his parents, his friends, his professors, and his girlfriend, he felt he had to get away from it all and find himself again.

Tony Campolo commended him. "That's a good thing to do!" he said. "But what if you start peeling away the layers of yourself, like an onion, and when you get rid of them you don't find anything at the center? What if you get to the heart of who you are, and you find there's nothing there? What do you do then?"

It's a tough question, one that most of us face at some point in our lives. Albert Camus wrote about that in his novel *The Fall*. A respected lawyer was walking the streets of Amsterdam one night. He heard a splash and then a cry for help. A woman had fallen into the canal! He began to run toward the splashing. But then his legal mind whirled into action: Someone should help her, but should it be him? After all, he had his reputation to think about. What would people say if she were a prostitute, or even another man's wife, and their names appeared in the newspaper together? Or, worse yet, a picture of him helping her? Would they think he'd been with her? What about his safety? Maybe some tough guys mugged her. Maybe they were still lingering in the shadows. Maybe they'd attack him, too, if he helped her!

He was deeply involved in his mental legal debate when suddenly he realized that the splashing had stopped. The cries for help had ceased. The woman had drowned. The lawyer wandered on, still playing the arguments in his mind, deliberating whether or not he should have tried to save her. He stopped at a tavern to drink himself into peace and used the person he found there as a father-confessor. Camus pronounced judgment on the lawyer in two short lines: "He did not answer the cry for help. That is the man he was."

We are each that person sometimes. That is what the Pharisees of Jesus day knew. Each person is a moral being caught in the quandary of ethical choices. Sometimes we make good decisions, sometimes we lean toward darkness and evil.

Their solution was to codify the divine standards given through Moses, and build walls of apparent behavioral "perfection" around themselves in the public eye. Through practice and protocol they managed to create a façade of holiness that breeched no impugnable offenses.

Once such "sanctity" is achieved, it needs to be preserved and protected. The easiest way to maintain "my" righteousness is to identify failures in others. Distract and blame. This is what they do with Jesus and his disciples, finding minor faults that raise their own sanctimonious quotient.

We do it too. Jesus knew this, as he addressed the rising shame and blamed poisoning the air. When the Pharisees set the rules of the holiness game, Jesus' own disciples thought they had to play accordingly.

That is why Jesus turned the tables on everyone. It was not the external that determines character, said Jesus. Even the best of moral projections can be driven by immoral hearts. We cannot, as the saying goes, determine a book by its cover.

In a parable by Kierkegaard, there was a break-in at a large store, but the thieves didn't take anything. When the clerks opened the store in the morning, all the merchandise was still there. A diamond necklace was marked $2,000, and a pair of leather shoes, fifty cents. A pencil, however, now cost $75.00, and a baby's rattle was priced at $5,000.

Instead of stealing merchandise, the thieves had stolen value. By stealing intrinsic worth, they had stolen *identity*. When the prices changed, no one knew any longer what the value was beneath the packaging.

Shelley Rodriguez, of Independence, Kentucky, explained the phenomenon this way. She brought her eight-year-old grandson to a farm. He loved the magic of the auctioneer's singsong voice, yet something bothered him. "Grandma!" he asked, "How's that man ever going to sell anything? He keeps changing the prices!"

Sometimes that seems to be the power of our society — changing the price tags on us, so we don't really know the value of things anymore. Society keeps changing the price tags of our identity, so we don't really know who we are. This is the crisis of identity. We're all trying to pretend, projecting more on the outside than we feel on the inside. In fact, sometimes the thing we're hiding most is something that's not even there — the emptiness of our own souls.

Influence Crisis

That brings us to the second major crisis of life. Dr. Erickson called it the *influence crisis*. What difference does my life make for others?

As parents, we want to influence our children. One pastor I know moved his family seven different times. During each of the last five moves, he left one or two children behind. As he retired, he was trying to figure out what had become of his family, and what impact his life had on his children. He mourned that the center was gone. They had no place to call home.

Parents make choices that affect the manner in which their children form their identities. Harry Chapin put it well in his song "Cat's in the Cradle." When he was a young father, he was too busy making a living to take time with his son. When he was finally old enough to enjoy time with the family, his son in turn had learned to be too busy for his dad.

Certainly, parents can have a positive influence, too. Maurice Boyd remembered one incident that sealed the impact of his father on his life forever. His father worked in a shipyard in Belfast, Northern Ireland. During the Great Depression, work dried up. Times were tough, and for three years his father was out of a job.

Then one of his father's old bosses at the shipyard approached him. The important man would find work for Mr. Boyd. He would guarantee it, no matter how much worse things got. All Mr. Boyd would have to do would be to buy a life insurance policy from the man. It would work to their mutual benefit: the boss's income would increase, and Mr. Boyd's work income would be guaranteed!

It was a great deal except for one thing: it was illegal. Maurice Boyd remembered his father sitting at the kitchen table with the whole family surrounding him. There at the table his father counted the cost. He reviewed their desperate financial situation. He ticked off the outstanding bills and the money he would be making, or *ought* to be making, if only he said yes to his boss.

His father wrote it all down on a sheet of paper: the gains and the losses, what he could make and what he could lose. Then he wrote down a category that Maurice Boyd will never forget: integrity. What did it matter if he gained the cash to pay the rent but lost his ability to teach his children right from wrong? What did it matter if he gained the dignity of a job but lost it each morning when he looked at himself in the mirror and knew that the only one reason he could go off to work instead of someone else was because he cheated?

His father declined the job, and the family groveled through several more years of poverty. Yet, of his father, Maurice Boyd said, "He discovered that no one can make you feel inferior without your consent, and that one way you can keep your soul is by refusing to sell it. He realized that whatever else he lost … he didn't have to lose himself."

Jesus put it this way: "What comes out of a person is what defiles them." Those who let the corruption stain their souls will defile their lives.

Yet it isn't a formula that we can play out in our lives through some program or recipe. Robert Coles, child psychiatrist and Harvard University professor, tried at one time to figure out why we do the things we do. In his book, *The Call of Service*, Cole reflected on people who try to make a difference in life. People who seek to reform themselves, even when sinful tendencies oozed like tentacles through their inner marrow. People who attempt to better society, in spite of the fact that it stubbornly refused the challenge.

Why do they do it? Cole asked. The people themselves often have a hard time defining what makes them tick. One young teacher in an urban school got challenged all the time by street-smart students. Weary of self-righteous do-gooders, they asked, "What's in it for you?" And he really couldn't say.

But all these compassionate volunteers have one thing in common: earlier in their lives, each of them ran into a crisis situation that tested their identity and their willingness to do something about it. In that crisis situation, each of them encountered someone who put his or her life on the line and taught them the meaning of service. They found someone who gave of themselves in a way that bucked the trend of selfishness and of self-preservation. The influence of that someone else made it possible for the person they helped to be greater than each of them had previously thought they could be.

That is greatness finding itself. Do you see it? In a troubled world, said Jesus, where the safest bet is self-preservation, perhaps especially in "religious" communities, we too often "…nullify the word of God by your tradition that you have handed down." That is why he pointed his disciples to a better path. Do you see them around you? Do you know the names of some whose last name is Father, and Son, and Holy Spirit? Do you know any "children of God"? Then you've been touched by greatness itself.

Crisis Of Integrity
The third crisis of life Dr. Erikson talked about was the crisis of integrity. The hardest thing to do in life was to maintain integrity. Sin had

entered the human soul precisely at this point. We are rather nice people, aren't we? There is much that we do that is good, fine, noble, kind, and wise, and no one can deny that.

But as with the Pharisees, that was precisely the problem: whatever else sin might do in our lives, it first and foremost perforates the lines of the heart, and allows us tear off a piece here and a piece there, until we find ourselves fragmented, torn apart in separate snippets of self. It isn't that we become blackened by sin in large strokes. It isn't that we turn into hideous monsters of greed and cruelty. It isn't that we dissolve the Dr. Jekyll's of our personalities into dastardly Mr. Hyde's. Rather, we keep most of our goodness intact, while making small allowances here and there. We cheat on our taxes a little, maybe. We turn our eyes from the needs of someone we could help. Or we compromise our communication until we speak from only our mouths instead of our souls.

The fragmentation of our lives makes us less than we should be, less than we could be. It makes us less than the people God made us to be.

There is a powerful scene in Robert Bolt's play *A Man for all Seasons*. The story is about Sir Thomas More, loyal subject of the English crown. King Henry VIII wanted to change things to suit his own devious plans, so he required all his nobles to swear an oath of allegiance that violated the conscience of Sir Thomas More before his God. Since he would not swear the oath, More was put in jail. His daughter Margaret came to visit him. Meg, he called her, with affection, was his pride and joy, the one who thought his thoughts after him.

Meg came to plead with her father in prison. "Take the oath, Father!" she urged him. "Take it with your mouth, if you can't take it with your heart! Take it and return to us! You can't do us any good in here! And you can't be there for us if the king should execute you!"

She was right in so many ways. Yet her father answered her this way. "Meg, when a man swears an oath, he holds himself in his hands like water, and if he opens his fingers, how can he hope to find himself again?"

You know what he meant, don't you? When our lives begin to fragment, it's like holding our lives like water in our hands, and then letting our fingers come apart, just a little bit. The water of our very selves dribbles away. We may look like the same people but who we are inside has begun to change.

"What comes out of a person is what defiles them," said Jesus, and we know what he meant. We are all of a piece. There's no separation in us between the impulse of the heart, the thought of the mind, the word of the mouth, and the action of the hands. Somehow, everything that we are is integrated. That is the meaning of the word integrity, isn't it?

But integrity is easily lost on us when we allow the shadows and shades to consume the unadulterated light of divine goodness within.

Conclusion

The beauty of life, though, is that each day we have a chance to start over. In some sense we are always on the brink of another year. It is said, "Today is the first day of the rest of your life." Let's imagine that there are 365 new days thrown back into the credit side of the ledger. What do we do with them? We know the law of averages. Those who tally our demographic lives tell us that each day 9,077 babies are born, 2,740 young people run away from home; 63,288 traffic accidents occur, in which 129 people die; 5,962 couples get married and 1,986 divorce; 500 million cups of coffee are consumed; and the snack bars at O'Hare Airport in Chicago sell 5,479 hot dogs.

And each of us is challenge in one of the three great crises of life:

- The Identity Crisis: Who am I?
- The Influence Crisis: What does my life mean to those around me?
- The Integrity Crisis: How deep is my soul?

Perhaps, because we remember the words of Jesus, the method to our madness will change. Perhaps a new motto will guide us, one also spoken by Jesus: "Seek first the kingdom of heaven, and all these things will be yours as well."

If that happens, we may change the color of society. After all, remember Martin Luther? Remember what happens when greatness begins to find itself? The world is never the same again!

Proper 18 / Ordinary Time 23
Mark 7: 24-37

The Price Of Popularity

There is an ancient legend first told by Christians hiding from persecution in the catacombs of Rome. It pictured the day when Jesus went back to glory after finishing all his work on earth. The angel Gabriel met Jesus in heaven and welcomed him home. "Lord," Gabriel asked, "Who have you left behind to carry on your work?"

Jesus told him about the disciples, the little band of fishermen, farmers, and homemakers.

"But Lord," said Gabriel, "what if they fail you? What if they lose heart or drop out? What if things get too rough for them and they let you down?"

"Well," said Jesus, "then all I have done will come to nothing."

"But don't you have a backup plan?" Gabriel asked. "Isn't there something else to keep it going, to finish your work?"

"No," said Jesus, "there's no backup plan. The church is it. There is nothing else."

"Nothing else?" asked Gabriel. "But what if they fail?"

The early Christians knew Jesus' answer. "Gabriel," Jesus explained patiently, "They won't fail."

It was clear to those around Jesus, as Mark told us, that Jesus was special. Demons fled and blind eyes saw. Jesus was powerful. Some of the religious leaders of the time, according to words preserved to this day (*Talmud: Sanhedrin* 43a), considered him to be a "sorcerer". Those who received his kindness and healings, however, saw the kingdom of God descending around them. In fact, there is in Mark's gospel, something scholars call "the Messianic secret." Several times over (as in 1:43-45, 8:29-30), and as is found in our passage, Jesus made a major splash with his divine authority, and it was about to become the talk of the town. But, "Shhhh....!" Jesus said. Don't talk about it. Why?

Precisely because his miracles were and are a big deal! In the politically charged atmosphere of his times, where the Jews were looking for a new Judas Maccabeus to lead an armed rebellion and get rid of the Roman occupiers, Jesus seemed a very likely candidate. He had the power. He commanded attention. He talked incessantly about the kingdom of God. Surely he was God's next great leader, rising up as deliverer like Moses, Joshua, or David.

Jesus could not do anything other than perform miracles and bring anticipations of the Messianic age. He cautioned those who wanted to lift him on their shoulders to make him king right then in a fit of mob madness, that was not the right time. Don't do it! The kingdom of God was on a roll, but its agenda unfolded piece by piece. Do not force me or it may become belittled by jumping ahead or taking only a small view of it, for your own purposes.

Yet the transformation brought by Jesus was apparent. God was doing a new thing on planet earth, and whether it was the Gentiles (like the Greek woman of Tyre) or the Jews of Galilee, people knew he was heaven's new messenger among them. They were amazed, and they kept talking.

As Mark's gospel continued, Jesus made it increasingly clear that a new age was dawning. He did miracles that pushed back the devastating effects of evil's contaminations. He brought anticipations of the new world being born out of heaven's graces. Those who joined Jesus in that campaign would do the same. In fact, one of the key messages of this gospel was that, while Jesus was with them for only a brief and shining moment, his work of transformation continues to unfold through the lives, actions, works, and miracles performed in his name by his disciples, then and now. The price of popularity, for Jesus and for us, involves several things.

You Can Make A Difference
The first is this: "You can make a difference." You can make a difference in the world around you.

Think of those to that Jesus was speaking and among whom he was performing miracles. It wasn't a gathering of the United Nations. It wasn't a conference of the superpowers. It wasn't a sitting of congress, parliament, or even an assembly at city hall. It was a woman in a hillside village and a man in a farming community of Galilee. It was a group of common people with no high ambitions or positions. In fact, they were under occupation. They couldn't make their own laws.

They couldn't plan their own futures. They couldn't determine their own destinies.

We are tempted to pass over the small and insignificant in society, dismissing them casually. Tony Campolo told of his friend who was walking through the midway at a county fair when he met a tiny girl. She was carrying a great big fluff of cotton candy on a stick, almost as large as herself. He said to her, "How can a little girl like you eat all that cotton candy?"

"Well," she said to him, "I'm really much bigger on the inside than I am on the outside!"

So it is with Jesus. And so it is with us.

Rallying against the usual helplessness of our mediocre days are stories of courage that remind us of the truth of Jesus' word. There's a marvelous little story tucked away in the pages of Edward Gibbon's seven-volume work *The Decline and Fall of the Roman Empire*. It told about a humble little monk named Telemachus living in the farming regions of Asia.

Telemachus had no great ambitions in life. He loved his little garden and tilled it through the changing seasons. But one day in AD 391 he felt a sense of urgency, a call of God's direction in his life. He didn't know why, but he felt that God wanted him to go to Rome, the heart and soul of the empire. In fact, the feelings of such a call frightened him, but he went anyway, praying along the way for God's direction.

Nobody heard him, so he crawled up onto the wall and shouted again: "In the name of Christ, forbear!" This time the few who heard him only laughed. But Telemachus was not to be ignored. He jumped into the arena and ran through the sands toward the gladiators. "In the name of Christ, forbear!"

The crowds laughed at the silly little man and threw stones at him. Telemachus, however, was on a mission. He threw himself between two gladiators to stop their fighting. "In the name of Christ, forbear!" he cried.

They hacked him apart. They cut his body from shoulder to stomach, and he fell onto the sand, with the lifeblood running out him.

The gladiators were stunned, and they stopped to watch him die. Then the crowds fell back in silence, and, for a moment, no one in the Coliseum moved. Telemachus' final words rang in their memories: "In the name of Christ, forbear!" At last they moved, slowly at first, but growing in numbers. The masses or Rome filed out of the Coliseum that day, and the historian Theodoret reports that never again was a gladiator contest held there. All because of the witness and the testimony of a single Christian.

You Can Make A Difference Together

You can make a difference. But Jesus added a second thing to it. We can make a difference *together*.

One disciple with a sense of purpose may make a statement in the world, but it's the community of Christians that turns the world upside down. The community made an impact. Others felt the leavening influence of it in the streets. The community of the church salted Romanian society, and it got a fresh taste, a different outlook, and a new character.

It is hard sometimes to imagine just how important community is. We like to think of ourselves as independent and strong, full of personal vitality. Yet often the first thing we hear from the lips of someone who is experiencing problems is, "Nobody cares. I'm all alone."

Some time ago I sat at a table with old friends. Years before they were the strongest Christians I knew. They loved the Lord; they loved their church; they were full of enthusiasm.

But this night, they were different. They were hurting and confused. They felt weak and tired spiritually. Why? Their congregation was torn apart, they said, and the people they sat next to in church were fighting one another. Their community had become a battleground.

My friends are still Christians, but their oldest son has stopped going to church with them. They have to drag the younger ones along and they have backed out of many ministry commitments that had meant so much to them in the past.

The community is gone, and with it went the power. The strength of their Christianity in testimony and witness has disappeared. When they talk about it, they sound tired. They are alone and slowly dying spiritually.

We can make a difference. But like the flicker of a thousand lights in the city on the hill, or the powerful taste of a spoonful of salt in the potatoes, we can do that best *together* — as a community.

You Can Make A Difference Together In The World

There's a third thing that Jesus tells us in his words and actions: we can make a difference together *in the world*.

I'm captivated by the events that surrounded the start of my own denomination, the Christian Reformed Church. One of our first pastors, the Reverend H.G. Kleijn, sent a letter to a Classis Holland meeting on April 8, 1857, telling the other church leaders that he was pulling out to start a new denomination. The church they were part of, he said, had too many contacts with the world around it. The church should be off by itself, separated from the rest of society, living its own little life in its own little corner. Here are his words: "The Church, the Bride of Christ, is a garden enclosed, a well shut up, and a fountain sealed."

Thankfully our denomination has gone well beyond the isolation of its early years and developed a strong evangelical witness. But Reverend Kleijn's view of the church has often intrigued me. Do you see his picture? The church is a nice little community off by itself, doing its own thing, untouched by the world. It is as pretty as a garden full of flowers, but it puts a high wall around itself so nobody else can get in. It is a well of refreshing water, but it is stopped up so nobody will get it dirty by taking a drink. It is a fountain of surging excitement, albeit sealed within concrete barriers, so its power won't slip away. That is the church, in a bad interpretation of Song of Songs 4:12, that Reverend Kleijn said he wanted to belong to.

But that does not seem to be the church that Jesus envisioned. The church is not just a little community off by itself somewhere. It is the confirmation that God still has an interest in our world. The Old Testament story of Lot and his family is instructive. Sodom was a wicked place; so wicked, in fact, that God *had* to destroy it. "Enough is enough!" God seemed to have mused.

But before God destroyed Sodom, he came down to earth and talked his plans over with Abraham. Lot was Abraham's nephew, and God wanted to make certain that Abraham understood what was going on. After they talked about it for a while, Abraham said to God, "I hear what you are saying. I know it is a wicked place. I agree, something has to be done. But what if there are fifty good people there? Would you still destroy it, even with fifty good people living there?"

"No," said God, "I would not. If there are only fifty good people living in Sodom, I will spare the whole city."

Abraham got his courage up. "But what if there aren't quite fifty good people there? What if you go down and count them, and you find only 45? Would you still destroy the city?"

"No," said God, "I reckon not. If there are only 45 good people there, I won't bring down my judgment on the place."

Abraham was on a roll now. He decided to press his luck. "Would you spare it for the sake of thirty righteous people?"

God probably sighed, but then said, "I guess I'd go that far."

In the end Abraham asked about twenty, and about ten, and God agreed to his terms. If only ten righteous people lived in Sodom, God would spare the whole city. The meaning was clear: the viability of a neighborhood is somehow tied to the residual influence of those who have a meaningful connection with God.

In the New Testament the apostle Peter picked up that same theme. He said there was enough evil in society, enough wickedness in our world, for God to let loose the fires of his judgment. But God is not going to do that yet, said Peter, because God has people living throughout the whole wide world, and they make a difference. They confirm God's relationship with this world. They are the salt of the earth.

What would our city be without our testimony? What would our region be like without the church of Jesus Christ? Where would our nation head without the conscience of the people of God? We are not to hide in a corner. We are not to hug ourselves within the walls of our pretty little garden. We are not to keep off by ourselves, hoping nobody notices us.

It is not enough to be anti-abortion; you must be pro-life and remind our community what real life, God's life, is all about. It is not enough to be against immorality; we must be the conscience of society, turning its thoughts toward love, laughter, and life. It is not enough to protect our own interests; we have to speak out for the welfare of the poor, the disabled, the oppressed.

We are the conscience of your society. God has placed us here as a symbol of God's continuing relationship with this world. We are the extension of Jesus' personality in this society. What difference does it make that we're here? Does anybody notice?

You Can Make A Difference Together In The World For God

Finally, we can make a difference together in the world *for God*.

It's not enough to be socially active, socially responsible, socially concerned. No mind is truly enlightened until it is flooded with the glory of heaven. Nobody is truly healed until it is touched by the power of the Creator. No person is truly set free until there is freedom of the Spirit of Christ.

William Carey was a pastor of a small congregation in Leiceter, England. In 1792, he preached a powerful sermon called "Expect Great Things from God; Attempt Great Things for God." People would remember it for years. His message not only moved hearts in his congregation, it also came home to challenge Pastor Carey's own soul. The next year he set sail for India and what he did in that country was simply astounding. He began a manufacturing plant to employ jobless workers. He translated the scriptures and set up shops to print them. He established schools for all ages, helping people find a better place in society. He provided medical assistance for the diseased and the troubled and the ailing. He was nothing short of a miracle for the people of India.

Why did he do it? When he lay dying, these were his last words: "When I have gone, speak not of Carey but of Carey's Savior."

There was only one reason for it all: You can make a difference in the world for God.

During the time of the Reformation, John Foxe of England was impressed by the testimony of the early Christians. He gleaned the pages of early historical writings and wrote a book that has become a classic in the church: *Foxe's Book of Martyrs.*

One story he told was about an early church leader named Lawrence. Lawrence acted as a pastor for a church community. He also collected the offerings for the poor each week, and that led to his death.

A band of thieves found out that Lawrence received the offerings of the people from Sunday to Sunday, so one night, as he was out taking a stroll, they grabbed him and demanded the money. He told them that he didn't have it. He had already given it all to the poor. They didn't believe him and told him they would give him a chance to find it. In three days they would come to his house and take from him the treasures of the church.

Three days later they did come. But Lawrence wasn't alone. The house was filled with the people of his congregation. When the thieves demanded the treasure of the church, Lawrence smiled. He opened wide his arms and gestured to those who sat around him. "Here's the treasure of the church," he said. "Here's the treasure of God that shines in the world."

There was a price that Jesus paid for his popularity. Not everyone knew it at the time. But the gospel will unfold that story, and point us in the same direction. We can make a difference together in the world for God.

Mistaken Identity

Appearances can be deceiving. Still, we often trust what we see more than what we read or hear. That is one of the reasons why television is so captivating. "Seeing is believing," we say.

Sometimes appearances can even change the way we think about things, and "deceive" us into a whole new attitude. Consider, for example, the report of Dr. Maxwell Maltz, a former New York cosmetic surgeon, who told of a magazine contest to find the ugliest young woman in the United States. Cruel as such a competition may seem, the magazine editors actually hoped to change the life of this unfortunate person for the better.

Photos poured in from all over North America. The editors selected a young woman with poor features, terrible grooming, and appalling clothes as the "Ugliest Girl in America." For her prize, she won a plane ticket to New York City. There a team of specialists went to work on her. Dr. Maltz reshaped her nose and built up her chin. Others gave her a new hairstyle, an elaborate wardrobe of the latest fashions, and grooming instructions. In a modern Cinderella story, the "ugliest" became quite beautiful almost overnight. Within a few months she was married.

In fact, says Dr. Maltz, the young woman's whole attitude toward life changed. Before the cosmetic transformation she had been shy and inhibited. She felt foolish, ignorant, and out of place in almost any company. But once she had tasted what she could become, her personality also exploded with new possibilities. She became confident and poised, articulate and informed. She attracted people to herself in any crowd.

Appearances can be deceiving. But who among us would be able to say which appearance was the deceptive one—the young woman whose photos won the "Ugliest Girl" contest, or the young woman who waltzed in beauty?

School On The Run

Faith is a matter of appearances as well. It is important that we understand who Jesus *is*, not just in our sometimes mistaken notions of who we would like him to be, but who he is by his own testimony and actions. That seems to be why Jesus challenged his disciples to read the appearances well as they walked one day in the north country of Palestine. "Who do people say I am?" he asked them.

The setting was quite appropriate for such a question, even if it does not immediately strike us that way from our first reading of the text. They were wandering in the region of Caesarea Philippi, we are told. This was a relatively new city built near the site of an ancient gathering place of spiritual significance on the slopes of Mount Hermon.

Mount Hermon is the highest point in Galilee, a striking conical dormant volcano that provides the only significant ski slopes in modern Israel. Because of its high altitude and its position in the northern regions of the land, Mount Hermon receives more rain on its slopes than do many parts of Palestine. The waters not only run down in creeks and streams, but they also sink below the surface to produce springs on the lower skirts of its foothills.

Near Caesarea Philippi there are springs and streams that create an exceptionally well-watered area. Trees grow in abundance and provide a shaded canopy filled with the sounds of gurgling and trickling waters, and a chorus of bird song. It is no wonder that Jesus would take his disciples there for a strolling Socratic teaching session.

But the place held more than just pleasant park-like settings. Because the waters bubbled and gurgled up from caves at the base of the mountain, area residents had long believed this to be the doorway into the underworld. Here, they thought, the spirits of the deep tried to communicate with creatures on the surface. Sometimes sulfuric gasses were emitted, and these only confirmed the presence of other-worldly voices and the breath of Hades.

Over the centuries, a variety of religious sects had used the place as a cultic shrine. They cut niches in the rock walls of the mountain just above the burbling caves and set up statues of gods they thought might be resident there. They even gave the place a spiritual name. They called it "The Gates of Hades." Here, they believed, was the doorway between the realm of the living and the abode of the dead. Those with keen faculties would be able to hear the whispers of the departed and the voice of the underworld gods. It was considered to be a very holy place.

But appearances can be deceiving, so Jesus comes with his disciples to test their perceptions. "Who do people say the Son of Man is?"

We ought not read too much into Jesus' self-identification here. Some thought he was making a divine claim already in the question that he asked his disciples. But it was more likely that Jesus was using the term "Son of Man" in a manner similar to that found in the prophecy of Ezekiel. According to Ezekiel, when he was approached by heavenly messengers to form a link in the communication process between God and God's people, the angels called him "Son of Man." The designation was more of a representational term than anything else. In effect, it was an acknowledgement that Ezekiel was truly human, but that he was being used in these settings as the conduit between the celestial and the terrestrial.

The "Son of Man," thus, was someone who had no unusual powers in himself, but who had been entrusted with a special revelation that was now supposed to be passed along to others. If Jesus used the term in this manner, he was merely asking his disciples what people thought about him, now that he had become a point of contact between them and God.

Identity Options: John?

So the answers came. "Some say John the Baptist," they told him. This was Herod's favorite and fearful line. Herod had long been fascinated with Jesus' cousin John, a wild man who lived outside the system. But John was also a prophet who criticized the system and those who ran it, and no one came under more of John's judgmental tirade than did Herod. Herod's forebears had taught him how to survive in politics: it was a matter of deception, bribery, murder, and power plays. When Herod dared to kill his brother and marry his brother's wife, it surprised few. After all, they had been carrying on an openly "secret" affair for year. Moreover, the new alliance produced political benefits for a variety of courtiers and solidified Herod's rule in territorial acquisition and the conferring of titles.

Herod wanted to get rid of John but he hesitated to kill the man. For one thing, John was a popular figure, and Herod didn't want to build too much resistance. After all, he fancied himself a true "King of the Jews," even if his ethnicity made that a huge stretch, and his religious devotion announced it to be a farce.

Fear of a popular uprising wasn't the only reason Herod didn't want to execute John. Herod was also superstitious enough to believe that John actually spoke for a powerful divinity. Herod was trying to play it safe. He was not about to garner more ire than necessary, especially if it came from transcendent sources. To have a powerful God against you was an unwise political bargain.

Still, John's public indignation against Herod, especially after Herod stole his brother's wife, was more than the king could tolerate. Herodias, too, disliked the man. She was at least as cunning as her new husband, and would not dismiss John quietly like some quack or minor irritation. Together they had John put in prison. Even there, however, the prophet refused to be silenced. Herod himself made many secret trips to see the man, now that he was so close at hand. And others who claimed to be John's disciples had ongoing access to their leader through sympathetic guards. The martyr-like John in prison was almost more powerful than was the former wild man of the Jordan valley. His mystique only grew larger.

Herodias devised a plan to push Herod into the executioner's chair. Using her daughter's beguiling dancing as a lure, she created a scenario where Herod had to buckle. At a heads-of-states banquet where Herod hosted his powerful friends, Herodias got her daughter to serve as entertainment, and then coaxed out of Herod a drunken public promise to reward her seductive whirling in any way she wished. Too late Herod realized his wife's part in the plot when it was John the Baptist's head the young woman demanded as payment (Mark 6:14-28).

Herod followed through on the recompense, for he had made a kingly vow. But since that time he had not slept well, believing that John would come back to haunt him. One may connive and kill others in the royal household, because that is the price of playing with power and living in its vortex. But John was an innocent from outside the system, and there would surely be divine retribution stalking Herod until blood was satisfied with other blood.

When Jesus showed up looking like John, sounding like John, and running an itinerant school of prophets like John, Herod was sure John had come back to do him in. This new John was probably even more powerful than his previous incarnation — hence the many miracles Herod had heard about — and was probably building a broad base of support to take Herod down in a very painful and public way. Herod believed Jesus was John reborn, and had great reason to fear.

But Jesus wasn't John, and the disciples knew it. They had seen John and Jesus together, and knew the one from the other.

Identity Options: Elijah?

There were other rumors about Jesus' identity floating around, of course. "Elijah" was a favorite among the scribes. They copied scripture and knew it well. Since every manuscript was a handwritten, labor-intensive work of faith, the scribes were committed to knowing every detail of the holy books and transcribing them accurately.

Among the many prophetic notes they painstakingly reproduced was the one left by Malachi. Five hundred years before, when some of the Jews returned from Babylonian exile, three men had stood to communicate God's new challenge to the restored community around Jerusalem. Haggai, the first of the prophetic trio, gave a divine word that was quick and specific. "Build the temple," he shouted to Zerubbabel, "for the Lord your God is with you!" In a few brief motivational speeches on two separate occasions Haggai served as the inspired cheerleader for this ragamuffin crew trying to pretend more strength than they felt in the face of overwhelming circumstances.

Zechariah was the second of the three most recent prophets. By way of apocalyptic visions Zechariah declared these days to be the harbinger of the end times. With smoke and fire and judgment God would soon come down to destroy all evil and to usher in the glory of the Messianic Age. It would happen right in and around Jerusalem, so those who had recently returned from exile should watch, wait, hope, and pray.

The final member of the post-exilic band of prophetic brothers was Malachi. His very name meant "my messenger," so he spoke unabashedly with the voice of God. When Malachi interacted with the crowds of Jerusalem what emerged was a dialogue in which God accused, the people responded with rhetorical questions, and God preached sermons of indignation against them. One of the questions the people asked of God was why God did not return to this temple they had rebuilt? After all, when Solomon created the temple that used to stand here, God showed up at the dedication service and flooded the place with God's own Shekinah glory presence. It was obvious that God had come to live in the temple.

But this time around God didn't seem interested in moving in. An earlier prophet, Ezekiel, had declared visions in which he saw the glory of God leaving Solomon's temple before the Babylonians finally destroyed it. Ezekiel had also predicted that the temple would be rebuilt, and firmly asserted that God's glory presence would re-enter the place. Now the temple was resurrected, however, and still God had not shown up.

Malachi boomed the opinion of God that the people did not really want God in the neighborhood. God would show up when the people were really ready to have God around. As a sign of God's good intentions, intoned Malachi, God would send another messenger to prepare the way. God would raise up Elijah of old, the first of the great prophets, and he would make things ready. Elijah would appear with stern speeches and mighty miracles. The people should get ready, for when Elijah came, God would follow quickly on his heels.

That is why some people thought Jesus was Elijah. Especially among the scribes who copied the prophetic writings this idea took hold. Jesus spoke with divine authority. He performed miraculous healings, just like Elijah had done. Maybe this was the occasion for God to fulfill Malachi's prophecies. If so, Jesus was the new Elijah.

But Jesus' closest disciples knew that was another case of mistaken identity. After all, Jesus had recently spoken clearly about the matter (6:14-15). He said emphatically that John the Baptist was the person that Malachi had written about. John was the new Elijah.

Identity Options: A Prophet?

Who, then, was Jesus? The disciples reported a couple of other rumors floating about. "Some say you are one of the other prophets."

Jeremiah was a fitting possibility. More than any of the other prophets Jeremiah entered scripture with a well-developed personality and a clearly articulated identity. He often reflected introspectively on his divine calling and the painfulness of his vocation. Jeremiah's friend Baruch added to the mystique by including biographical information into the record that contained Jeremiah's prophetic tirades.

Moreover, Jeremiah did not disappear from the scene easily. At the end of his prophecies he urged the remnant remaining in Jerusalem to stay there and rebuild. But they were fearful of a return visit from the Babylonian armies, so they kidnapped Jeremiah and forced him to march with them to Egypt. It was at that point that Jeremiah slipped into the hazes of history. Many believed that soon he would recover and roar again out of the fog of time. When Jesus quoted Jeremiah's prophecy on several occasions, many were quick to pin the ancient seer's name on this new man of God.

Yet Jesus knew better than anyone else that he was neither John nor Elijah, neither Jeremiah nor another of the prophets come back to life. He put the matter squarely to those who shared his meals and his snoring and his daily dusty walk, "But who do *you* think I am?"

It was Peter, of course, who answered. Peter was like that boy who sat in the front row of our third grade class. Our teacher would treat us as if we obviously knew what she was talking about. The problem was, we usually didn't. But none of us dared admit our ignorance, believing we would be the butt of every ridicule for the rest of the year.

Not so the boy in the front row. He was already out to lunch in our books and we loved to hate him for it. When our teacher told us things she expected us to know, he would raise his hand and ask her why or what she meant. She would patiently explain everything again more elaborately, and we were in our childhood glory — we got from her what we needed but were too afraid to ask, and we got from our naïve classmate someone to razz for being so stupid.

So with Peter. The rest of the disciples don't really know what to say. Can they call Jesus a miracle worker? Should they say he speaks with a prophet's voice? Dare they admit they think he might be Messiah?

All their fears of communication faux pas were put to rest when Peter jumped too quickly into the embarrassing silence and blurted out that Jesus was the Christ, the Son of the living God. But there was no satisfaction there, for the answer was more troubling than the question. As long as Jesus was merely interested in public opinion this discussion was a pleasant way to pass time and share a place in the spotlight of success. But now that Jesus had demanded clarification from them, they could not hide behind other skirts.

The Familiar Stranger
What should they say? How do you live with someone in the intimacy of the kind of relationship they have had with Jesus and yet linger on the fringes of mistaken identity?

Jesus was their familiar stranger. He was the man who lived down the hall, yet remained an enigma. The disciples knew they didn't really know him, yet they were willing to live with the tension as long as nobody had to name it. We are not that different from them.

One of the college courses I often teach is called "Which Jesus?" In it I take my students through Jaroslav Pelikan's book *Jesus through the Centuries* (Yale, 1999) plus the writings of the New Testament, and reflect on the variety of ways in which people think about Jesus. Each time I teach this course I ask my students to write a paper that requires that they talk with their parents about how Mom and Dad view Jesus. Invariably I get some papers still wet with tears from students who never before knew the Jesus of their parents' religious devotions. Too long they had passed by one another snickering at the religious folly of others while never having to face the question of Jesus' identity themselves.

Somehow Peter had learned enough during his time as a student in Jesus' rabbinical school to get the answer right on the oral exam. Somehow he managed to sift through the files of mistaken identities and come up with the declaration that Jesus is more than a prophet, more than a religious curiosity, more than a spiritual guru superstar. Jesus is the Christ, the Son of the living God. Jesus brought heaven to earth and earth to heaven. Jesus is the link between imminent and transcendent, and all of us need to know that if we are to get firm footing on the rock that really matters.

With the wall of religious trends there at Caesarea Philippi framed in the background, Jesus affirmed Peter's testimony. None of these other superstitions, commonly known as the "Gates of Hades," spanned the gap between heaven and earth. They never do. We reach, hope, hedge our bets, and pray. But unless we know the identity of Jesus, our religious actions are like bad gas burping from the caves of an old volcano.

So the question Jesus asked back then is always relevant. "Who do you say I am?" Do you know?

Majoring In Minors

Some time ago I was riding a train through central England and a man boarded at one of the stops. As he looked for a seat, he saw my face and beamed at me with great joy. "Hi Will!" he said brightly, in a wonderful British accent.

Unfortunately I'm not Will. When he sat next to me and I opened my mouth to protest his mistaken notion of who I was, my flat American English paved the way for his embarrassment. Obviously I was not the person he expected. Nevertheless, we got along "brilliantly," as the British put it, and I am no longer either Will or a stranger to the man.

Mistaken identity is not all that uncommon, especially when there are only so many variations to our same facial features. After Albert Schweitzer and Albert Einstein gained worldwide fame, and had their pictures printed in a variety of media, some mistook the former for the latter. Once Schweitzer was approached hesitantly by a mother and daughter duo who asked if he was the great scientist Einstein. Rather than disappoint them, with more magnanimous grace than he felt, Schweitzer signed an autograph, "Albert Einstein by way of his friend Albert Schweitzer."

Or take the case of Queen Elizabeth II of England. She was stopped once in Norfolk as she entered a tea shop. Two women were exiting carrying baskets of cakes and breads. One commented to her that she looked remarkably similar to the queen. "How very reassuring," said the modest royal personage, and moved on. Her daughter, Princess Anne, had a similar encounter. At a sporting event she was approached by a woman who said, "Has anyone ever told you that you look like Princess Anne?"

She replied, "I think I'm better looking than she is."

Mistaken identities may commonplace, but on some occasions they are more serious than others. Certainly that is true in Matthew 16. Just before these verses Jesus had asked his disciples what people were saying about him. Did they get it right? Did they know who he was?

They gave back a variety of answers, and Jesus didn't seem too surprised. But to his disciples' chagrin, neither did he drop the matter there. Instead he pressed the query home in a very personal challenge. "Who do *you* say I am?" he demanded.

There was no room for fudging on this exam. Jesus had made it intense and immediate. No time to go back to the books for a night of cramming.

Fortunately for the others, Peter blurted out an answer: "You are the Christ, the Son of the living God." Fortunately for Peter, he got it right. Jesus praised him on the spot.

Strange Reaction

That only made this next scene so weird. First, Jesus changed the mood of the conversation too quickly. One moment they were grinning and enjoying that moment when friends reach a new level of insight, commitment, and trust; the next Jesus was rambling on about death and dying. It didn't fit. Peter, certainly, wanted to bask in his celebrity status for a while. After all, he had managed to give the right answer to the toughest, most embarrassing challenge Jesus could have thrown at them. It was like winning an Oscar and a Grammy all at once, and Peter wanted to spend more time at the podium receiving the accolades of both Jesus and the others.

But Jesus stepped up to the microphone and started recording his martyr's testimony. He was going to Jerusalem, he said. He knew his enemies were waiting for him there. He was certain they would arrest him, beat him, and make him suffer. He was confident that the outcome of their actions would result in his death.

There was clearly some kind of incongruity there. Peter had just voiced the great testimony that made Jesus seem invincible. And in the next breath, Jesus was breathing defeat and disaster. How do these match up? Where is the connection?

Stranger Response

If that wasn't enough, things only took a more eerie turn. Peter knew he had deal with this. After all, Jesus had just identified him as the leader among the twelve. Furthermore, he was still confident about knowing the right answers. So he pulled Jesus aside and started to talk him out of this morbid reflection. "Look here, man; you're scaring us. Do you hear what you're saying? You better get it together, Jesus. This is getting out of hand."

At that moment Jesus roughly pushed Peter away and started shouting at him. "Get away from me, Satan!" he yelled. "You're standing in my way! You're blocking my path! You're fighting against God!'

The disciples were in sudden shock, and Peter most of all. He was so taken aback that he didn't know what to do with himself. What could have caused this sudden tirade?

Everyone stood around for a bit, looking kind of dumb. Then Jesus broke the silence but with a different demeanor. He poured out his heart. He gave them a sense of what was ahead for him, and for them. And in those moments of conversation, Jesus spoke to them about the meaning of life. It is a strange and paradoxical word, but one of the truest things they would ever come to know and we with them.

Don't Stop Here

For one thing, Jesus told them that life is a journey, not a destination. You see, when Peter made his testimony, his confession, his blubbering statement about who Jesus was, there was a sense of euphoria in the group.

You know how it is. Remember when you first said to someone that you loved her? Remember how those words changed everything? You didn't know if you should say it. You wanted to, but then again, you didn't want to.

But suddenly the words blustered out and smashed into the open space between you. They took over. They stopped the conversation. There was nothing more to be said. You just sat there and looked at one another. It was like time stood still. This is the moment! Make this moment last!

That is what Peter and the others were feeling when he blurted the words for the first time. "We think the world of you, Jesus! You're the Son of God! We love you! We didn't know who we were until you came along!"

When they talk that way, they want to sit around for a while and just smile at each other. The moment was intense and it begged to consume all those in it.

Rabbi Harold Kushner remembered a scene from a television program that he saw years ago. He said it showed a young man and a young woman leaning together against the railing of a ship at sea. The winds tussled at their hair. The sprays showered them now and again. But they didn't notice any of it, because their eyes were glued on each other. The world disappeared around them as they murmured their love.

"If I should die tomorrow," he said softly to her, "I'd have lived an eternity in your love."

She nodded her head in bashful intimacy and leaned over to kiss him. Their lips lingered and they became one as the bustle around them faded. Finally they slipped away, arm in arm in the waltz of passionate lovers.

Behind them, in the void left as they shuffled the slow two-step to the left, the camera caught a life preserver hanging on the galley wall. It carried the name of the ship: TITANIC.

Maybe, in our soap-operish television viewing, that is enough for them: one night of romantic passion. That is the stuff of legends and fairy tales, where everything is compressed to the great hour of heroism or the night of intense love. Prince Charming kisses Sleeping Beauty and everything else gets summarized in a single line: "…and they lived happily ever after." Or the heir to the kingdom finds Cinderella and the rest of the story is just one sentence: "…and they lived happily ever after."

That is often the way we want it, in our books and movies and television programs. We want to linger in the critical moment. We want to feel the emotional high of the kiss in slow motion. We want to sit in the experience of the warm fuzzies and then go get a burger.

But Jesus said no. Jesus said that life isn't found in the moment, not even if it is a moment of insight, love, or passion. Life is a journey, not a destination.

It is always tempting to settle down into that special moment, though, and try to make it last. When Phil Donahue wrote his autobiography he told of something that happened to him in decades ago, in his early years of broadcasting. He was a reporter for CBS at the time, and they sent him to Holden, West Virginia, in the heart of the Appalachian Mountains. Holden was a coal town where everybody worked the mines. News media were gathering that day because a mine shaft had collapsed trapping 38 men underground.

Rescue teams rushed down as the clock ticked out the anxious limits of human survival. The weather turned bitterly cold. It took three days to clear the passageways and get within striking distance of the ensnared men. Finally, at 2 am on the morning of the fourth day the first of the desperate miners cleared the surface and stumbled out of the mine entrance.

Families gathered tightly to hug each new survivor. Snow fell over them in the circle of temporary lights as the local pastor called them to huddle around a little fire. He led them in a prayer of thanks for the rescue. Then they held hands and sang "What a Friend We Have in Jesus."

Donahue said it gave him goosebumps. It was *so* beautiful. He told the cameramen to roll the film, but the sub-zero temperatures had frozen the mechanism and they were not able to record anything.

Phil Donahue is not a man to let a golden opportunity to slide by, so he grabbed the pastor aside and asked him to do it all again—the prayer, the song, the spiritual passion. Donahue wanted to make the feelings happen all over again. "We have 206 television stations across the country," Donahue told him. "Just let us get another camera and you can share this moment of faith with millions."

What happened next astounded the fledgling reporter. The pastor shook his head and said, "Son, I can't do that. We've already prayed to God. We can't do it again. It wouldn't be right."

But that's what Peter wanted, wasn't it? That's what the other disciples desired as well. With Phil Donahue they wished the moment of truth to linger. They craved for the passion to last. They wanted to hold hands and speak kind words and sing those songs of love. They begged for the cameras to roll, and then they hoped to play the video over and over and over again. That's when Jesus reminded them that life is journey, not a destination.

That can be frightening for us because we get used to a moment of great beauty and then want to hold on to that moment. We try again and again to recapture it in some way, and relive it as if it were more real than the rest of our humdrum hours.

It is for that reason that traditions latch onto us. They can become for us reminders of a moment in the past when things seemed so right in our world: a Currier & Ives Christmas, for instance, or an illuminated Thomas Kinkade painting glowing with just the right moment of sunset perfection outside and the warmth of faith and family shining through the windows of a still life home. G. K. Chesterton called tradition "the democracy of the dead." He said that when we fell in love with tradition we handed the current moment over to voices and times from the past. Let them tell us what to do. Let's try to relive the good old days. "The democracy of the dead."

But life is a journey, said Jesus. "If anyone would come after me he must deny himself and take up his cross and follow me."

That means traditions alone cannot keep our faith strong. It means that life, society, and the church will always be changing. It can be frightening to us. How often I have had conversations with people who wished to turn back the clock, to put the pages back on the calendar, to relive the past once again. Then everything would be right, good, true, and noble.

But it cannot happen. Soren Kierkegaard put it straight when he wrote that if we are really honest we experience fear when we read these words of Jesus. "Follow me!" he called. But where? And how? And in what way?

Why can't we just stay in the little huddle, feeling good about ourselves? Why do we have to hit the road with him?

Kierkegaard said that we should really collect up all our New Testaments and bring them out to an open place high on some mountain top. There we should pile them high and kneel to pray, "God, take this book back again! We can't handle it! It frightens us! And Jesus, go to some other people! Leave us alone!"

Still Jesus stands next to us, sandals on his feet, staff in his hand, and says to us, "Time to go, folks." Life is journey, not a destination. And we know he is right.

Journey With Purpose

There is something more as well. Jesus tells us that life is a pilgrimage, not a tour.

You know what a tour is, don't you? It's where you let someone else do all the planning. They take care of your luggage. They put you on a big, air-conditioned bus and ferry you around to all the right sights. They pay the entrance fees for your tickets so you don't have to stand in the heat or the sun or the smell by the booth. You can stay safe, comfortable, and dry, while others do the sweating for you. That's a tour.

When I studied for a semester in Israel we watched tour groups come through in regular fifteen-minute intervals. We were studying history, archaeology, and biblical geography, so we walked, hiked, and followed paths that weren't paved. But the tour busses swept by with tourists who saw Palestine from their windows and never breathed the air or felt the wind or sneezed the dust. Clean in, clean out.

A true pilgrimage, however, isn't like that. A pilgrimage is always personal, always firsthand, always something you have to do yourself. That is what Jesus said to his disciples. With Peter they want him to watch God's plans work themselves out from a safe distance. They wish for him to rest with them on the sidelines, to take the tour on the big love boat instead of swimming with sharks.

But Jesus said no. Life is a personal journey. He could not avoid it. He could not have someone else stand in for him. He had to make the pilgrimage himself.

Walter Wangerin Jr, put it powerfully in his allegory of Jesus as the Ragman. Wangerin pictured himself in a city on a Friday morning. A handsome young man came to town, dragging behind him a cart made of wood. The cart is piled high with new, clean clothes, bright, shiny, and freshly pressed.

Wandering through the streets the trader marches, crying out his strange deal: "Rags! New rags for old! Give me your old rags, your tired rags, your torn and soiled rags!"

He saw a woman on the back porch of a house. She was old, tired, and weary of living. She had a dirty handkerchief pressed to her nose, and she was crying a thousand tears, sobbing over the pains of her life.

The Ragman took a clean linen handkerchief from his wagon and brough it to the woman. He laid it across her arm. She blinked at him, wondering what he was up to. Gently the young man opened her fingers and released the old, dirty, soaking handkerchief from her knotted fist.

Then came the wonder. The Ragman touched the old rag to his own eyes and began to weep her tears. Meanwhile, behind him on her porch stood the old woman, tears gone, eyes full of peace.

It happened again. "New rags for old!" he cried, and he came to a young girl wearing a bloody bandage on her head. He tooks the caked and soiled wrap away then gave her a new bonnet from his cart. Then he wrapped the old rags around his head. As he did this, the girl's cuts disappeared and her skin turned rosy. She danced away with laughter and returned to her friends to play. But the Ragman began to moan, and from her rags on his head the blood spilled down.

He next met a man. "Do you have a job?" the Ragman asked. With a sneer the man replied, "Are you kidding?" and held up his shirt-sleeve. There was no arm in it. He could not work. He was disabled.

But the Ragman said, "Give me your shirt. I'll give you mine."

The man's shirt hung limp as he took it off, but the Ragman's shirt hung firm and full because one of the Ragman's arms was still in the sleeve. It went with the shirt. When the man put it on, he had a new arm. But the Ragman walked away with one sleeve dangling.

It happened over and over again. The Ragman took the clothes from the tired, the hurting, the lost, and the lonely. He gathered them to his own body, and took the pains into his own heart. Then he gave new clothes to new lives with new purpose and new joy.

Finally, around midday, the Ragman found himself at the center of the city where nothing remained but a stinking garbage heap. It was the accumulated refuse of a society lost to anxiety and torture. On Friday afternoon, the Ragman climbed the hill, stumbling as he dragged his cart behind him. He was tired, sore, pained, and bleeding. He fell on the wooden beams of the cart, alone and dying from the disease and disaster he has garnered from others.

Wangerin wondered at the sight. In exhaustion and uncertainty he fell asleep. He lied dreaming nightmares through all of Saturday, until he was shaken from his fitful slumber early on Sunday morning. The ground quaked. Wangerin looked up. In surprise he saw the Ragman stand up. He was alive! The sores were gone, though the scars remain. But the Ragman's clothes were new and clean. Death had been swallowed up and transformed by life!

Still worn and troubled in his spirit, Wangerin cried up to the Ragman, "Dress me, Ragman! Give me your clothes to wear! Make me new!"

We know the picture. It was the one that Jesus described to the disciples that day on the road. It was an allegory of the pilgrimage he was on, the journey that is always personal, the path that could not be watched from a distance. Jesus was the Ragman who had to touch lives, who must heal wounds, who was bound by necessity to bring relief. This was the pilgrimage of the Ragman to the center of the city, to the garbage heap of society, to the hill called Golgotha—the Skull! The place of death! The mountain of the crucifixion! There he must go. Personally.

No Spectator Sport

So too those who are with him. Religion is no spectator sport. Harry Emerson Fosdick remembered a storm off the Atlantic coast. A ship floundered on the rocks and the Coast Guard was called out. The captain ordered the lifeboat to be launched, but one of the crew members protested. "Sir," he said in fear, "the wind is offshore and the tide is running out! We can launch the boat, but we'll never get back!"

The captain looked at him with a father's eyes, and then said, "Launch the boat, men. We have to go out. That is our duty. But we don't have to come back."

So it is, in one of the strangest things about life that Jesus told us here. The one who wanted to protect himself, the one who wanted to hide herself, the one who wished to guard himself carefully, will never find the meaning of life. "Whoever wants to save his life will lose it. But whoever loses his life for my sake will find it."

That is why Jesus was so angry with Peter. Peter wanted Jesus to take the easy way out. He wanted Jesus to save his own life, to guard his own safety, to keep his body intact. But how could the Ragman not be the Ragman? How could the Son of God not be the Son of God? How could Jesus not do what only he could do?

Do you know what the early church leaders said about Peter? They had a legend about him, and something that happened in his later years. They said that at the time of the great persecution under Nero the Christians of Rome told Peter to leave. "You're too valuable," they said. "Get out of town! Find your safety! Go to another place and preach the gospel."

According to the legends Peter is supposed to have gone from the city. Yet only a few days later Nero had Peter in custody. Soon afterward he was sent out to die. When the soldiers took Peter to the site of execution Peter begged of them one last request. He asked that he might be crucified upside down. He said he wasn't worthy to die in the same way as his Lord. So they nailed him to his cross inverted.

Then, according to the stories, the crowds of Christians gathered round. They wanted to be with their beloved leader as he died. "Why," they asked him as he hung there upside down on the cross, "why did you come back, Father Peter? Why did you return to Rome? Why didn't you flee into the hills?"

This was what Peter was supposed to have said. "When you told me to leave the city I made my escape. But as I was going down the road I met our Lord Jesus. He was walking back toward Rome, so I asked him, 'Master, where are you going?' He said to me, 'I am going to the city to be crucified.' 'But Lord,' I responded, 'were you not crucified once for all?' And he said to me, 'I saw you fleeing from death and now I wish to be crucified instead of you.' Then I knew what I must do. 'Go, Lord!' I told him. 'I will finish my pilgrimage.' And he said to me, 'Fear not, for I am with you.'"

That is the end of the story for us today. Peter's great confession; Peter's great denial; and Jesus taking both into his great heart, turning them into great grace. Life is a journey, he told us, not a destination. We cannot sit down at one spot, however lovely it might be, and hug ourselves into some "…happily ever after."

Moreover, life is a pilgrimage, Jesus told us, not a tour. It is lived in the footsteps of the Master. It is pursued in the purposes of the Ragman and his associates. It is carried out in the mission of the church.

Here is the road no one wants to travel. Yet if you choose not to walk it, you will never find yourself.

What does this mean for you personally? I don't know. I can't know for you and you can't know for me. But this I do know: I know that you will know what it means for you if Jesus has spoken to you today.

Heaven's Culture

Here is a great poem by Edwin Markham:

> He drew a circle that shut me out —
> Heretic, rebel, a thing to flout.
> But love and I had the wit to win:
> We drew a circle that took him in! (In the public domain)

It's beautiful, isn't it? In the face of attitudes that would kill, "love and I had the wit to win: we drew a circle that took him in."

The heart of what Jesus told his disciples in Mark 9:38-50 was essentially that loves reaches out. John, Jesus' own best friend, his "kindred spirit," the man who thought his own thoughts after him, wanted to draw lines of separation: he's not one of us! We told him to cease and desist! We are "in" and they are "out". But Jesus redrew the lines, and gathered others into the family. This is heaven's culture.

Sometimes we point to people like Adolf Hitler, shake our heads, and call him a murderer. And we should. There is no excuse in the world for what he did. He was a murderer, and we all know it.

But Jesus forces us to take one step further. He talked to us about circles of death and circles of life, circles that shut people out of our lives, and circles that bring them in. The act of murder, Jesus said, is merely an attitude that has come full circle. And, unfortunately, that attitude grows in all of us, even in Jesus' best buddy, the "Beloved Disciple."

At the end of World War II, the great German theologian Reinhold Niebuhr said, "We must finally be reconciled with our foe, lest we both perish in the vicious circle of hatred." That's the kind of thing Jesus told us here.

But righteous indignation against people like Charles Manson and Jeffrey Dahmer is never enough. The murderer is not just a strange and twisted figure out there. The murderer also lives in each of us.

Certainly, death isn't always murder, nor is it always painful. I remember the Friday evening when one of my grandmothers died in Minnesota. She was almost 93 years old. My Dad called and said that it was a great thing for her to go home to be with the Lord. Death was a welcome doorway into eternity. She once told me that one of her favorite verses in the Bible was in the final chapter of the Song of Songs. The whole book is about love and is summed up in chapter 6 this way:" Love is strong than death!"

Questions for us, as we listen to Rabbi Jesus, include: How is love stronger than death? What is it that we win when we draw circles of love instead of hate, of inclusion rather than exclusion?

I Win A Brother

For one thing, we win a brother. We win a sister. We win a friend. This is the story in our text that starts the whole conversation. John saw the other man, spiritual as he was, powerful enough to wield heaven's power against demons, as an enemy. "Us" versus "them", and "he" is not one of my "brothers".

Jesus challenged that thinking.

In a rural community where I once lived, there were two brothers who farmed together. One was a bachelor and the other was married. For many years they had worked together, one running the dairy, one taking care of the land. Things went along just fine. Then the bachelor brother got married to a beautiful woman. Shortly after that a baby came along.

That led the brothers to start thinking about the future. Maybe it was time for them to split the operation so that each family could have its own share. And that was when the trouble began. It seemed easy enough to divide the land and the machinery. The cow herd was a bit more difficult. Since one brother had worked with these animals for years, he knew each, and understood their temperaments and their production capacities. He split the herd in half, and each brother had a new barnful of the cows. But after a couple of years, one herd began to produce much more milk than the other.

The brothers did not talk about it, other than to note the facts. But one of the wives felt cheated. She was sure that the other brother must

49

have gotten the better cows. She complained. It didn't take long before her husband went to his brother in a huff. Obviously, his brother had worked it out somehow so that he got the best producing cows. He had cheated his own brother!

That is when the fights began. They started calling each other names. They used to sit next to each other in church during worship services each Sunday, but now they began choosing opposite doors and opposite sides. One of the couples called an elder and me, as their pastor, to come over. "Tell them they're doing wrong," they said about the other couple. "Force them to give us a better deal!"

Then one wife stopped coming to worship services. And when her husband's term as deacon was finished, he left the church, too. They never came back.

Who won? Nobody.

Who lost? Everybody. The brothers each lost a brother. The children lost respect for their parents. The church lost members, and Christ lost his people. They started it all with little accusations that drew lines between "us" and "them". In the end, only the fires of hell were the richer.

Maybe that is an extreme case. Still, we know that the same thing plays out in other communities, and in every human heart. We draw circles around ourselves constantly: the circle of pride, the circle of jealousy, the circle of bitterness.

There are fourteen words in the Bible that have the meaning "to kill someone intentionally." Several of them speak of thoughts of the mind and attitudes of the heart rather than acts of the hand. One word means "to devalue" another person until that person has no worth. A woman remembers something that happened years ago. Someone hurt a friend of hers. Later, the man in question became her Elder at church, but she wouldn't let him visit. She wouldn't even talk with him. She drew a circle, and he was on the outside. Because of it they both lost.

Another word used in the Bible means "to separate" myself from others. A man sat with a load of bitterness. Someone had done him wrong. He was never going to forget it and neither was anyone else who came near him. The circle was drawn, and every year it got tighter.

Who wins? No one.

But when love reaches out past hurts, something astounding happens. A psychologist named Kinch described it this way, back in 1963: Five graduate students in psychology at one university, he said, created a rather bizarre experiment. They were part of the "in" crowd at the university. They moved in the right circles. They dressed the right way, had the right friends, and went to the right places.

They decided to focus their attention on one young woman who wasn't in that circle. She was an outsider, a nobody, a person who didn't count, at least to them. Normally they wouldn't even talk with her. Yet, for the duration of the experiment, these fellows agreed to treat her like she was one of their crowd, like she was a somebody. They decided to talk with her, to call her up, and to ask her out. They made an agreement that whenever they saw her, they would complement her and show an interest in her.

After a little while, as they carried out this experiment, something strange began to happen. She became more likable. She became less foreign, less alien.

The first fellow's date with her was hardly bearable. He had to keep repeating to himself: "She's beautiful. She's beautiful. I've got to keep telling myself that she's beautiful." By the time the third fellow asked her out, however, she had become part of their circle of friends. It was kind of fun being with her. She wasn't so bad after all. And the fifth fellow never did get to date her because the fourth fellow in line asked her to be his wife. (*American Journal of Sociology* Vol. 68, No. 4 (January 1963), pp. 481-486)

That may have been a cruel experiment at the beginning, and certainly not something to try again, but isn't it amazing what can happen when we redraw the circles of our lives?

> He drew a circle that shut me out —
> Heretic, rebel, a thing to flout.
> But love and I had the wit to win:
> We drew a circle that took him in!

What do I win in the circle of love? I win a sister. I win a brother. I win someone who is my friend and ally.

I Win A Father

In verse 41, Jesus told of a second thing that we win in the circle of love, and that is heaven's blessing. We win our Father.

Think of a person who came to the temple to worship God. She brought her offering. She gave it to the priests who would burn it as a sacrifice. She knew that her prayers would be heard by God in heaven, just as the smoke of the offering drifted toward the skies.

Yet somehow, that time, it didn't seem to work. Her religion was useless. Her prayers bounced back from the ceiling. Her songs sounded empty and hollow, and God was silent.

Did you ever feel that? Did you ever feel like God was off on holidays, and things around you operated randomly, all meaningless?

A close friend to Elvis Presley remembered a time shortly before the singer's death. Elvis was in the music room, with the volume turned way up as one song played over and over: "How Great Thou Art."

The man asked Elvis, "How are you doing?"

Elvis answered with a single word: "Lonely."

Lonely. That seems to be the picture Jesus paints, isn't it? When we have left things undone between ourselves and others, somehow we cannot find God either.

The great preacher William Holmes used to tell the story of a beggar who came to the door of a magnificent mansion and asked for a bit to eat. "Go around to the back," he was told. There the master of the house met him. The gentleman carried a plate of food. Since he was a Christian, he wanted to set a good example, so he told the beggar, before he ate, that first they must ask for God's blessing.

"Just repeat after me," he said. "Our Father."

"Your father," said the poor man.

"No, no!" said the master of the house. "Let's try it again: 'Our Father.'"

"Your father," said the beggar again.

"No!" said the rich man. "Didn't you hear me? I said, 'Our Father!'"

"Well, sir," answered the other man, "I figured that if I said, 'Our Father,' that'd make you and me brothers, and I'm not sure the Lord would like it, you makin' your brother come beggin' at the back door for a scrap of bread."

That's true, isn't it? In fact, later in the New Testament, the Apostle James wrote, "Religion that God our Father accepts as pure and faultless is this: to look after the orphans and widows in their distress ..." (James 1:27). He reminded us that in some way, when we draw a small circle around ourselves and keep others at a distance, we keep God away from us, too.

Jesus said essentially the same thing in one of his parables. He said that at the end of time, when we face the Father, he would talk with us about the way we treated those around us in this life: the poor, the lonely, the outcast — the ones that are shut out from the "pleasant" circles of life. He will look at us with loving eyes, and he will tell us of the ways that we reached out to him. "Whatever you did to the least of these," he will say, "you did to me as well."

But some of us will blush and burn at that moment. We will remember those lines: "You drew a circle that shut me out — Heretic, rebel, a thing to flout." And the eyes of the Father will be sad. Then we will know what we have missed in life. We will have lost a lot of brothers and sisters. But we will also have lost our Father in heaven.

"There are no ordinary people," said C.S. Lewis in one of his sermons. "Next to the Blessed Sacrament itself, your neighbor is the holiest object presented to your senses." When you win your neighbor by lengthening the circle of your love, you come closest to touching God himself.

I Win Myself

There is a third thing that Jesus spoke about in verses 43-45. When you expand your circle of love, you win a brother, you win a sister, you win a father, and you win yourself as well. Jesus makes it clear: when you draw the circles of fear, hatred, and bitterness around yourself, the one who gets hurt the most is you.

Ibn Saud was the first modern king of Saudi Arabia. He lived during the early half of the twentieth century, and people in the East still talk about his wisdom. One day a widow came to him in a rage. She wanted justice against the old man who had killed her husband. The story was strange: her husband had been walking under a palm tree when the other man, up in the tree gathering dates, slipped and fell on him. Her husband eventually died from internal injuries received in that accident.

Ibn Saud checked the matter out and found it was true. He asked the widow, "What compensation will you take?"

He thought that she would want a pension in order to care for her family in the years ahead. But instead she asked that her husband's unintentional killer be put to death. She wanted the other man to die. She drew a circle that shut him out.

Ibn Saud knew that her family needed support, not revenge. Quietly and calmly, he tried to talk her out of it but she was adamant. Her husband was dead, and his slayer must die, too. There was no way to get her off her singular track.

When he saw that his coaxing was useless, Ibn Saud tried one more thing. He agreed to the death penalty, but he decreed that it be carried out in a very specific way. The man who killed her husband, he said, would be bound and set under a palm tree. Then the widow herself must climb the tree and throw herself down on the man, killing him.

"But I might also die!" she protested.

"Yes," said the king, "but hasn't your thirst for revenge already destroyed your soul? Aren't you just as dead as you wish him to be?"

The widow relented. She let the man live, and she received back her own life.

In much the same way, Jesus said here that when you create an adversary, in the end, you will always be the loser. Frederick Buechner wrote that anger was the most fun of the seven deadly sins. Anger makes you feel like you're feasting on a banquet fit for a king: you lick your wounds; you smack your lips over grievances long past; you roll over your tongue the prospect of bitter confrontations to come; you savor to the last morsel the pain you are given, and the pain you give back.

There is only one problem. In the end, when the meal is over, you find that you have eaten yourself. You have consumed your own flesh, and you are the one who has died.

There is a wise saying in the Hebrew Talmud: "A person who carries a grudge is like a man who accidently cuts one hand with a knife, and then stabs his other hand because it slipped." Imagine a hunter skinning his game with his hunting knife. He holds the warm flesh with his left hand while he slits the skin with the knife in his right hand. But the knife slips and cuts deep into his left hand. Blood spurts and the hunter shouts in pain.

What is he likely to do? Will he clean the wound and bandage it? That would be wise. But imagine the hunter instead becomes angry with his right hand for causing the wounds to his left. His left hand gropes for the fallen weapon and stabs his right hand, returning pain for pain, avenging the first cut with a deeper gash. If we were to watch this incident, we would roll our eyes at such idiocy.

Yet, in some way, this is what Jesus is trying to tell us. If we carry a grudge against someone who offends us we are not seeking healing; instead we are replaying the hurt to bring greater pain. We are as foolish as the hunter, more maimed than if we had sought healing instead of revenge. If I react to hurt by paying someone back tit-for-tat, then, as with the hunter, two wounds bleed instead of one, and no healing can begin. I lose my brother, and I lose something inside myself that becomes monstrous against him. Only when love and I have "the wit to win," when we draw "a circle that [takes] him in," do I gain something of myself back again.

Dale Galloway told of a friend who had a very shy son named Chad. The other children didn't usually include Chad in their circle of friends. Every afternoon his mother saw the school bus stop and all the children pile off in groups, laughing, playing, and joking with each other. Chad would be the last to come down the steps, always alone.

One day in late January, Chad came home and said," Know what, Mom?" Valentine's Day is coming, and I want to make a card for every single person in my class!"

Chad's mother felt terrible. She thought Chad was setting himself up for a fall. He was going to make valentines for everyone else, but nobody would think of him. He would come home all disappointed and just pull back further in his shell.

Still Chad insisted. So they got paper and crayons and glue. Chad made 31 valentine cards. It took him three weeks. The day he took them to school, his mother cried. And when he came off the bus, alone as usual, no valentine cards from anyone else in his hands, she was ready for the worst.

But Chad's face was glowing as he marched through the door triumphantly. "I didn't forget anybody!" he said. "I gave them all one of my hearts!" (Dale Galloway, *Dream a New Dream* [Wheaton: Tyndale, 1975]).

That day Chad gained something more than friends. He gained himself. He won a sense of dignity and worth.

That is how Jesus wants us to live. Circles of hatred erased by circles of love. Circles of bitterness blurred by circles of caring. Circles of death that give way to circles of life.

Isn't that what God has done for us? "While we were still sinners," said the Apostle Paul, "Christ died for us!" (Romans 5:8). When we had drawn God out of circles, God's love drew us in. When we counted God as our enemy, God called to us as his friends. When we hardened the walls of our hearts against God, he softened us with his love.

After all, couldn't that poem be the conversation of heaven, the talk between the Father and the Son about you and me?

He drew a circle that shut me out —
Heretic, rebel, a thing to flout.
But Love and I had the wit to win:
We drew a circle that took him in!

Love is stronger than death. The day Jesus drew a circle of love that took us in is the day death died. We are free to live and draw circles like our Savior.

Proper 22 / Ordinary Time 27
Mark 10:2-16

Bonding And Confidence

I had lunch one day with a pastor of a neighboring congregation who wanted to welcome me to the community. We were old friends and had a great time reminiscing and catching up. That night, when we were talking together as a family about the things we'd done during the day, my wife Brenda asked me where we had crossed paths before.

"Well," I said, "his sister was my first girlfriend."

Of course, *that* got the attention of a few ears. "Daddy?" asked one of our daughters, "did you think a lot about girls when you were a teenager?" I had to admit that I did.

There was no stopping this thing now, "Mommy?" came the next question, "did *you* think about boys when you were a teenager?"

"Yes," said Brenda, "I did."

They were on a roll now. "Mommy and Daddy, why do teenagers like each other so much?"

What do you say?

I remember what Chuck Swindoll said one time. He was speaking at a conference, and one morning a woman handed him a note. In it she told him that she had gotten married at the age of 31. She said that she hadn't been worried too much about being single until then, although she did have a rather peculiar practice. Every night, before she went to sleep, she hung a pair of men's pants on the headboard of her bed. Then she knelt next to her bed, held onto the trousers with one hand, and prayed this prayer:

> Father in heaven, hear my prayer,
> And grant it if you can;
> I hung a pair of trousers here —
> Please fill them with a man!

That's a good story, but something happened to Chuck Swindoll that makes it even better. He shared this story with his congregation the following Sunday morning. The crowds, of course, roared with delight. Chuck did see one young man who didn't smile. In fact, he seemed a bit preoccupied.

The young man's mother wasn't in church with the family that morning, having stayed at home to take care of a sick daughter. But a couple of weeks later, the mother slipped a note to Chuck after worship. It read, "Dear Chuck, I am wondering if I should be worried about something with our son. For the last two weeks I have noticed that before he turns out the light at night he hangs a woman's bikini over the foot of his bed ... Should I be concerned about this?"

Why do boys and girls like each other so much? What should we say? Certainly, when Jesus reflects on marriage, he has some things in mind about human sexual relations.

Human Sexuality Is The Best Thing That Ever Happened To Us

First, the Bible indicates that our sexuality is the best thing that ever happened to us. In the story of creation, God fashioned Adam to roam his beautiful new world. God brought all of the animals to him to play with, but they were not enough. Adam was alone in a crowd, so God created Eve to be with Adam, someone like him in every way and yet so different.

In that act God declared that loneliness was bad — so bad that it did not belong in a world that God declared "very good." The way to get around loneliness is to find a relationship that matters with a person who matters. God intended for that to happen by making us gendered beings who find deep attraction to one another.

Don't imagine that Adam was a prude. Don't think that Eve was shy about being a woman. Don't pretend that Jesus didn't understand what it was like to be male. After all, he was one of the three persons of the holy Trinity of God who said together, at the beginning of time, "Let us make humankind in *our* image, ... male *and* female."

That does not mean that the persons of the holy Trinity of God are male and female; rather, it reminds us that the persons of the Trinity had such a wonderful relationship together that they wanted others to share whatever was good about it. When they scattered the stars and the planets across the universe, and when they condensed the moisture of the earth into seas and clouds, and when they planned together the human form, they must have said to one another: "We have got to give these humans the delightful relationship we share with each other."

The best way they could figure to make that happen was to endow some of us as females and others us up as males.

God declares, at the beginning of time, that the best thing that can happen to us, humanly speaking, is our sexualized identity.

The Purpose Of Our Human Sexuality Is To Find Deeper Identity

But Jesus was not just talking about human sexuality in these verses. He also addressed the major threats to marriage: adultery and divorce. In what Jesus said, he affirmed the sanctity of marriage. He shouted in a large voice that marriage was holy. Jesus declared that there was something very special about marriage, and that *no one* ought to tamper with.

Why is marriage such a sacred thing? It has to do, in part, with our search for self. Notice that when Jesus spoke of someone committing adultery, he gave the impression that that person didn't really comprehend the outcome of his or her actions. The same is true with the person who divorces. Divorce means somebody wasn't in touch with the self. The person divorcing does not understand what this action means for all the parties involved.

We come into this world as *unfinished* creatures, works in progress. Little babies are fully human, but no one would say that they are fully developed. They have a lifetime of potential growth and development ahead of them. Intellectually, they will need teachers to pour waters of learning into the sponges of their minds. Volitionally, they will need parental discipline to shape, mold, and give contour to the persons they are becoming. Socially, they would respond to friends and communities, until they found a way to be themselves in relation with others.

Still, chances are that they will not truly find themselves in a very personal way without help from someone of the opposite sex. Says A. E. Houseman:

> When I was in love with you
> > Then I was clean and brave!
> And miles around the wonder grew
> > How well I did behave! (public domain)

He was saying that something of himself came alive *only* when he found himself in relationship with another.

I remember how it was when I "fell in love" for the first time. No one understood me like she did! Definitely not any of my other friends! Certainly not my parents! *I* didn't even understand myself as much as *she* understood me! One of the most fascinating parts of our courtship was our conversations together. We could talk about *everything*. She helped me understand who I was just because she was there for me.

Renowned psychiatrist Rollo May said in his book *Love and Will* (New York: Delta, 1969) that loving a person of the opposite sex and finding intimacy with that person has five deepening dimensions to it. Some of them are relevant to us here.

First, he said, there's a tenderness that happens to us which softens our hard walls of self, and which penetrates the mighty defenses we use to protect our individuality. Remember the old song about love that Jimmy Dean made popular? It spoke of a giant man who was brought to his knees by falling in love.

So it is with us. Our individuality makes us scramble for a personal identity. At the same time, our sinfulness makes us fight for our distinction from everyone else. But something about love burrows past our rocks, walls, our pride, and opens us to the wonder that there might be in intimacy with that special person.

Second, said Rollo May, there is the affirmation of myself in a relationship of love. Social scientists talk to us about the culture of space. We each draw a circle around us wherever we go, whatever we do. In North America, that circle is about three-to-four feet wide. It extends from the center of the body approximately eighteen inches to two feet in every direction. It is the space we claim for ourself, the space we "own" as we move in this physical realm.

The circle is our "personal space," and we will not easily allow someone else to enter it. Notice this next time you are in a crowd. Most people will keep others about eighteen inches to two feet from the centers of themselves. And if someone should be so bold as to invade our space, what do we do? A nice person will lean slightly away from the other person, or perhaps take a step back. A child or rude adult will give the other person a good push back into his or her own space.

In different societies the size of the circle changes. In Nigeria, where we served as missionaries, the circle was much smaller — only about two feet wide. But every culture has personal space that is guarded with great tenacity.

We guard our space because we are afraid someone else might dominate our identity. We are afraid another person will overpower who we are. We are afraid that we will lose our sense of self if someone else comes too near.

What happens to us when we fall in love? Suddenly we cannot get close enough to our beloved. It has been said that the scientific term for holding hands is "premarital interdigitation." It is part of that closeness that we allow only to someone special. "Here," we say," you can come into my space. That's right. Come on in. Here, let me hold the door for you. Sure, come right on it."

The only reason we can do that is because in love we know the other person affirms us, rather than seeking to annihilate us. That is the second thing love means to us: it affirms who we are.

The *third* dimension of love, said Rollo May, is the creative element. There is something about love which convinces us that together we are more than the combination of our individual selves. I give to you. You give to me. And somehow in the giving a greater identity is formed.

A friend of mine during our college years found this to be true. He was part of a group that included about fifteen or so companions, two-thirds of which were female. They treated one another as sisters and brothers, never actually dating within the group. One young woman was a particularly close confidant to my friend. They took long walks together, sharing everything.

Then one day someone began courting my friend's female companion. Suddenly his conversations about her changed. They still walked, talked, sat, and went for coffee together or with others of the group. But my friend became excited about her in a way that he had not before. It was not that he wanted to date her, although I think some fires of jealousy were kindled at times. Mostly, though, it was that energy created through her blossoming relationship with another fellow that brought out dreams, goals, insights, and a zest for living that astounded him. He thought he knew her so well, but then suddenly began to glow even brighter. Because of love, her qualities of personhood stretched in wonderful new ways.

God beautifully confirms the creative energy of lovers through the blessing of children. In a real sense, children are the two selves of the parents that come together to form a greater new self.

The *fourth* dimension of love is closely tied to the third. It is the giving dimension. Love teaches us the truth of Jesus' statement, "It is more blessed to give than to receive" (Acts 20:35). Giving is the beginning of receiving where love is concerned. Why do lovers give each other gifts? Is it to buy back something in return? You know it's not. Lovers give because it is the meaning of love itself.

Read C.S. Lewis on love sometime. In *The Four Loves*, he explored the four Greek words meaning love that were available in Jesus' day. There is *storge*, which means kind thoughts and affection. It is the type of love children have for pets. There is *philia*, which is the tenderness of friendship. Third, *Eros* always has a physical dimension to it.

And then, said Lewis, there was also a little-used term: *agape*. Nobody was using it much anymore, but somebody forgot to take it out of the dictionary. Along came Jesus and the church, and they suddenly shouted it everywhere.

Agape means a love which reaches beyond the warm fuzzies of itself and seeks to bring life and joy and delight and meaning to another person. *Agape* is the Bible's word of love. "We love," says John, "because God first loved us" (1 John 4:19). The word John uses is *agape* — the giving love. The love that reaches beyond itself to touch another life with beauty. When the other dimensions of love are there, according to Rolla May, the fifth and final dimension happens. It is the dimension of shared consciousness.

Poet John Betjeman remembered a sacred moment in a tiny tea shop in Bath, England. He sat at his table and watched an elderly couple enter. They took a booth nearby and ordered a pot of tea and some crumpets. Then he recorded their conversation in his own words:

> "Let us not speak, for the love we bear one another —
> Let us hold hands and look."
> She, such a very ordinary little woman;
> He, such a thumping crook;
> But both, for a moment, little lower than the angels
> In the tea shop's ingle-nook. (In the public domain.)

This is a picture of the intimacy of love when identities begin to fuse. It is what the Apostle Paul meant when he said, "Have this mind in you which was also in Christ Jesus ..." (Philippians 2: 5). For the deepest dimension of love is to share, beyond the physical realities, the consciousness of the other.

God made us males and females because we would only be able to plumb the depths of ourselves more fully when we found ourselves in relation with that other person. We call it culture. When you start learning the culture of another human, and the language that expresses it, you begin to better understand your own language.

So it is with our human sexuality. Many have noted that the language of males seems to be of one kind, while the language of females is another. In some sense males can never really understand their own language, with all its hidden culture and biases, until they learn something of the female lingo. Similarly, females can never really understand their own language until they learn something of the male lingo.

In fact, the more each of us has the ability to learn of the other language, the more we begin to understand our own native speech. We begin to understand the culture of our own hearts as we find our deeper identity through relationships, most often across the gender divide.

Our Greatest Need In Finding That Identity Is Love And Safety

Our greatest need in finding that identity is love and safety. This is why Jesus said very pointed things about adultery and divorce. No one in this world knows me better than my wife, and no one in this world has helped me to know myself better than Brenda has. The reason we have gained access to each other has to do with safety. I can share bits and pieces of myself with many people. I can share moments and thoughts with close friends. But with Brenda, I'm learning to share everything that I am in all five dimensions of love.

How does a couple develop that intimacy? Like this: Brenda has created a safe place for me. Our marriage is a sanctuary of safety where we can express and explore those dimensions of love. If I am to enter her space, if I am to gain access to a place that allows me to find my truest self, if I am to learn the female language in order to understand my own native tongue, then I have to know that she will not violate me. She will not ridicule or demean me, she will not destroy me, she will not use me and toss me aside, and she will not abuse our intimacy.

If I am to find myself, I need to know that she wants me to find myself, and that she wants to find me as well — not to abuse, but to cherish.

This is where we fulfill our greatest sexual need: within the sanctity of marriage. Dr. Nancy Moore Clatworthy, a professor of sociology at Ohio State University, spent ten years researching people who lived together without being married. When she began her research, she was convinced that living together was a good thing, perhaps even a better thing than the stuffiness of marriage.

Yet she wanted to prove it in a scientific way. For that reason, she interviewed hundreds of couples who were living together, observing the development of people as their lives unfolded.

Amazingly, in spite of her own wishes, she found that living together without marriage is one of the worst things for the human person because the context of safety is gone. People who move in together view the relationship as non-committed sharing, so they can never fully give themselves to the other person in the relationship. Why should I give myself to you if tomorrow you can walk right out of here? Why should I trust you with my intimate self if I don't know whether you'll protect me when you find me?

Dr. Clatworthy now vehemently opposes co-habitation outside of marriage. She says that our human sexuality *demands* the safety of marriage in order for us to become the persons we can be, the persons we are supposed to be.

Other studies confirm Dr. Clatworthy's research. The results of a scientific survey were published in Canada under this title: "A Hazard Model Analysis of the Covariates of Marriage Dissolution in Canada." It said that those who choose to live with someone of the opposite sex before marriage were twice as likely to have the relationship end in divorce as those who did not cohabit first. Why? Because if this is a trial relationship, I will never be able to believe that you won't walk out on me. The possibility of finding the safety to be my truest self is gone.

This is why Jesus had such strong words about adultery. This is why Jesus had such strong words about divorce, because they kill the spirit without ending the life of the body.

Sexual Perversions And Adultery Are Serious Crimes

That is also why sexual perversions are such serious crimes: domestic violence, incest, and rape. Each of them cuts at the heart of our human identity. Each of them violates the safe space we need in order to find ourselves. Each of them robs us of something essential to our characters.

The first question we ask when a child is born is this: "Is it a boy or a girl?" Our sexuality is as basic as our human existence, and when someone steals away from us something of that sexual identity, our very lives are demeaned!

That is why Jesus uses such strong language for anyone who presses that edge. In another passage echoing these thoughts he cries: "Cut your eye out! Saw off your hand!" If you take someone's car, you can pay them back. But if you violate someone's sexuality, you destroy something of their very souls. You can never undo the damage.

I hope that message is clear. The best that can happen to you, most often happens to you as a sexual person. And the worst that can happen to you, might well happen to you as a sexual person. God meant for you to enjoy your sexuality to the fullest. In fact, only in sexual relationship with another person will you begin to find your truest self. That is why Jesus cautions us to deal wisely with each other in sexual relations, because the greatest violence that can happen to someone happens when we violate him or her sexually. Don't let it happen!

We, as males and females, have often grown embattled against one another in our society. Christ can break down the barriers between us. Where we are presently engaged in activities that would harm others or ourselves sexually, Christ can help us overcome the worst evil in our souls. Where we have been horribly wronged by others and where we have horribly wronged others, Christ can lead us through the hurting and healing steps of forgiveness. Where our marriages have ended in divorce, Christ can give us a second chance to find sexual meaning and intimacy and identity. Where marriage is not a possibility for us, Christ can make our lives full and complete in ways that transcend even our sexuality.

The human race is like a radio. It can make a lot of noise, and it can produce a lot of music, but the best sounds come in stereo — female and male. And the best music happens when the system is tuned to the frequency God designed for it.

Inverted Reality

Twenty-six letters might be good enough for most people, but for Dr. Seuss, that was just the beginning. In his book *On Beyond Zebra*, one of Dr. Seuss' great little characters takes the reader on a tour of life beyond "Z is for Zebra." It was a whole new world of creatures most of us have never seen before. Things run on different time schedules, and life itself has a very different feel about it in the world *On Beyond Zebra*.

Jesus did something similar in Mark 10:17-31. A good man came, looking for a simple answer. After all, Jesus was increasingly recognized as a "rabbi", a reliable teacher regarding theological matters and ethical questions. The man was a good man, and always trying to be better. Maybe his conscience bothered him. Maybe someone had challenged his business practices. Maybe his relationship with another person was coming undone, and fingers of blame were being wagged.

We do not know all of the background to this simple interchange but it is recorded for us, because we all feel the same at times.

Think of it like this: your friend tells you that she's cutting a class and sneaking out to the beach for an hour. What do you say? "Hey, I'm coming with you!" Or maybe, "Do you think we'll get away with it? Do you think we'll get caught?"

You see, there some standard by which you judge your actions. Maybe it's by the rules of the school. Maybe it's by the laws laid down by your parents. There is always some norm by which we judge our actions — Is it right? Is it legal? Will I get away with it?

For the people of Jesus' day, it was the law and the prophets of the Old Testament. The rules and regulations of the Hebrew scriptures told people how to live. So Jesus placed these quickly before the man.

Most people thought these were enough. Take the Pharisees and the scribes, for instance. The law and the prophets were enough for them. That was how they regulated their lives. They felt no need for anything more.

But Jesus did not tread lightly on those religious leaders. In fact, Jesus went on to say some pretty harsh things. "I tell you," he said, "unless your righteousness *surpasses* that of the Pharisees and the teachers of the law, you will certainly not enter the kingdom of heaven."

And here he turned the tables on this devout seeker. "Sell all you have," Jesus told him. "Give everything to the poor!' The man walked away, but his frown lingered. Said Jesus: "Children, how hard it is to enter the kingdom of God! It is easier for a camel to go through the eye of a needle than for someone who is rich to enter the kingdom of God."

Wow! What did Jesus mean by that statement? Jesus' own disciples were dumbfounded! Was not wealth a sign of God's blessing? Did not the rich care for the many poor? Were the wealthy not responsible for building synagogues and repairing the temple? How could the kingdom of God be closed on them?

What did Jesus want of them, of us, of anybody? This man was only trying to live a perfect life. What kind of demands was Jesus painting for us in the land on beyond perfection?

We Go Beyond Saying Yes To Understanding No

One of the things that Jesus was saying to us is this: in the land on beyond perfection, we go beyond merely saying yes to understanding the meaning of no.

Our daughters were perfect examples of that. No matter how fast they were growing up, it was never fast enough for them. They saw adults, and they thought that we had it so good. They could not *wait* to be grown up so that life will be wonderful for them too.

What is it that makes adults' lives seem so wonderful? It is probably a combination of a number of things, but most important among those is this — they thought that *we* could do so many more things that *they* could. *We* could stay up later. *We* could watch whatever programs we wanted to on television. *We* could drive cars and go wherever we wanted. When *we* went to the grocery store, buy whatever *we* wished, even all the junk food *we* could pile in the cart.

There are so many things that we can do as adults that children cannot. They have to go to bed on time. They have to practice piano. They have to go to school. They cannot eat just anything they want.

They look at us and think that it must be *wonderful* to be an adult. To be able to say yes to so many fun things in life. And they know that someday, when they grow up, they'll be able to *anything* they want to do. Right?

Wrong.

When we finally grow up and at last have the legal right to do anything we want, life itself changes us. Other kinds of laws take over. Maybe your parents won't say "no" to you anymore, and maybe even the laws of the government won't stop you from doing some things. But you begin to learn that the only true way to say yes to anything in life is by learning how to say no to something else.

Sure, you can eat anything you want. That also means, however, that you can't wear the clothes you used to wear. Sure, you can stay up as late as you want. But that also dictates that you can't do other things you might have thought about doing the next morning. Sure, you can have sexual relationships with as many people as you can get into your bed, but the other side of that truth is that you can't have intimacy with anybody.

Somehow, the quality of our lives is found as much in our ability to understand the meaning of no as it is in our wonderful capacity to say yes. I once asked a pastor that I had known for many years how things were going for him in his retirement.

"Wayne," he said to me, "I have never enjoyed life so much. I'm just as busy now as I used to be, but it's different. I found this wonderful little word that I'd forgotten how to use. It's the little word spelled 'N-O'."

He went on to say, "I'm finding out just who I am again, because I'm learning how to use the word *no*."

During the Middle Ages, theologians used to debate questions like how many angels can dance on the head of a pin, or where does the soul come from when a child is born, or can God create a stone too big for him to move?

While those issues may be interesting diversions, the problem with such inquiries is that they forget that this is a moral universe. The question is not whether God can do something bigger than God can control, but whether God will do something which is outside of God's moral character.

You see, there are some things God *can* do, because God is God, but he *won't* do, precisely for the same reason: because God is God. When God says to you, "I have loved you with an everlasting love. I will always be there for you. You can count on me. I will never leave you or forsake you," then God is saying yes to you in letters as big as the heavens. But God is also saying, "No, I will not let the evil in this world grab hold of you forever. I will not allow even death to snatch you away from me. No matter what may happen, child, I'll never let go of your hand."

That is why Jesus said that he didn't come to destroy the law and the prophets. The law and the prophets were God's way of hanging onto God's people. They were the powerful "no" to sin and evil and death that framed the great "yes" of God's love for us.

So when Jesus wanted us to travel with him to a land on beyond perfection, he was reminding us that no great *yes* is ever shaped apart from its line of definition.

Who are you? You know it by the lines you draw.

We Go Beyond Legalism To Liberty

Learning the meaning of no isn't enough. A cartoon ran in *The New Yorker* some time ago. The scene showed a man at the gate of heaven. He had just died, and now he was carrying on a nervous conversation with the Apostle Paul. There were beads of perspiration running down the man's face. He was wringing his hands in anxiety as he tries to give a good account of his life, just like the young rich man who approached Jesus.

Peter, however, was shaking his head. "No, no, no!" he said. "That's not a sin either. My goodness! You must have worried yourself to death!"

The morality of Jesus is more than just lines of definition. Yet this is precisely how the young man, along with his crowd, likely Pharisees, saw their religious lives.

Who were these Pharisees and teachers of the law that demanded definitions? They have gotten pretty poor press over the years. Nobody seems to think anything good about Pharisees. Just look at the stories in the gospels. A Pharisee went up to the temple to pray. He stood up there in all his pride and thanked God that he was not an ugly, sniveling creature like that despicable tax collector over there.

Or think of the time that Simon the Pharisee invited Jesus to his house for dinner, only he forgot to have Jesus' feet washed at the door. He forgot to treat Jesus with respect and he laughed about Jesus' acquaintances to his friends sitting at the table. You get the idea — that Pharisees were rather rude people.

Later, when we find out that they were in on the plot to kill Jesus, it does not polish up the picture we have of them too much, does it?

But if we dig into the history books we can find out a little more about these strange people. The first book we turn to is the rest of the New Testament. Who was the Apostle Paul before he became a Christian? He was a Pharisee! He told us that being a Pharisee meant two things to him: a godly lifestyle and a belief in the resurrection.

In fact, when Paul was on trial one time (Acts 22), and they asked him what he believed, he looked at the Pharisees in the room and said he was still one of them. He still believed the things they believed, while he was already a Christian. Paul could be a Christian and a Pharisee at the same time. Pharisees were good people.

When we turn to the writings of Flavius Josephus, we get a similar picture. Josephus was the great historian of the Jewish people at the same time that the New Testament was being written. Josephus tells us about Pilate and Herod, and even mentioned Jesus a couple times. He also tried to explain to the Roman rulers the contours of Jewish society — who's who and what's what. When he mentioned the Pharisees, he saidthat they were the best of Jewish people.

Indeed, he said that when he was a young man he personally lived for a time with each of the major groups within Jewish society: the Sadducees who cared for the temple; the Essenes, who lived pure and separate lives out in the wilderness; and the Pharisees. Guess what? Josephus became a Pharisee and remained one for the rest of his life. Whenever he talks about the Pharisees, his words glow. He considered the Pharisees beautiful people. They cared about others. They cared about the quality of life. They were not rich, most of them, but they were wealthy in the things that mattered.

The Pharisees, Josephus wrote, tried to live as God's people in all things. All of Jewish society looked up to them.

When you read Paul and Josephus, and their contemporary, Philo of Alexandria, you get a rather nice view of the Pharisees. In fact, if you try to translate the picture into today's world and the Christian church, this is the kind of person you might find calling himself a Pharisee:

- He would have grown up in a poor but pious home.
- His parents would have sacrificed to send him to a private Christian school.

- He would be married, with children, and they would have devotions together at mealtime.
- Every week they would attend worship together, and he would serve a second term on the church leadership board.
- He would sacrifice to send his children to Christian schools.
- His wife would be a volunteer at the local chapter of Right to Life.
- He would attend Promise Keepers meetings and conventions.
- He and his wife would vote for conservative politicians who would promise to recover God's ways and blessings in America.
- As a family, they would support a Third World child through and international aid organization.
- They would contribute a tithe of all their income to the church.
- Every year at least one week of vacation would be spent volunteering in some mission project.

That's what a Pharisee would look like today. Why, then, did Jesus have such a dim view of the Pharisees?

Actually, Jesus probably did not. But Jesus knew that whenever people began to live good lives, like this pious young man, there was a danger that they would start realizing it. That is the moment when whatever is morally upright in their lives became skewed, twisted, and ugly. The danger of that happening is greater for nice people and that was what Jesus saw in the young man.

I had a friend at college who I thought was a great person with his head screwed on straight. He was one of the most genuine and caring persons I had ever met. It was quite a thrill when, after graduation, we both found summer jobs in the same city. We located two more roommates and rented a house from a professor who was going to be out of the country for the summer.

There we were, living together, going to all ball games, sitting out on the porch on those lazy summer events, shooting the bull. But it almost killed our friendship. I thought so much of him that when we became housekeepers together, sharing so much time together. I told myself, "Mark is an awfully good guy, and I think a lot of him. I'd better be on the best behavior. I don't want him to get upset with me."

Meanwhile, Mark was thinking the same thing about me. So here we were, two friends, and yet we were dancing this little dance around each other: "Whatever you like." "Sure, I'll do that for you!" While we were looking at how to be nice, we forgot how to be real. When we forgot about being real with each other, we lost the very thing that made our earlier friendship so special.

That is the problem for *good* people. Once they grow in their goodness, it is easy for them to begin to focus on being good.

Professor Ed Dowey of Princeton Seminary showed how easy it is to slip from grace to legalism. He remembered strolling down a street one day, preoccupied with his own thoughts. Suddenly a young girl met him and gave him a smile so bright he couldn't help but feel the warmth and energy she brought into this world. He didn't know her and there was no other reason for them to connect except that they shared the sidewalk together. "It was a moment of grace," he said.

Then a funny thing happened. The next day he happened to be on that sidewalk again and he found himself looking ahead at faces pushing toward him to see if that same young girl might come his way this day as well. Yes! There she was again! Immediately, said Dowey, something changed inside of him. Without thinking he edged toward her path before she even knew he was there. Then, as soon as she caught sight of him he shot her a huge smile and a friendly greeting. He still didn't know her, he said, but it seemed like the thing he had to do.

When he reflected on the incident later it occurred to him — what had been a moment of serendipitous grace that first day had captured his desire like a sweet treat. The second day he maneuvered to make it happen again. Rather than waiting to receive some little blessing from a stranger, he now tried to influence the circumstances in order to coerce another smile. The grin he received the first day was grace, commented Dowey, but the one he earned through manipulation on the second became a kind of legalism. To all outside appearances the actions were entirely unchanged from one day to the next. Inside, however, Dowey said, something had altered. He had tried to take a good thing and then buy it back again to recapture the feeling.

The morality of the world on beyond the perfection of the Pharisees and other nice people, says Jesus, is a morality that somehow manages to go beyond legalism to liberty. In other words, it is a morality that remembers that the other *person* is more important than the day to day *activities* of our relationship. If I love my wife, Brenda, I should talk with her, spend time with her, do nice things for her, protect her, and plan evenings with her.

But it is also possible for me to talk with Brenda and to spend time with her and to do nice things for her and to protect her and to plan activities with her and yet, at the same time, to let the meaning of our relationship slip away.

So it is in our relationship with God. The harshest words Jesus had were directed as "good people," like the young man who walked away, and the many devout wealthy, pious people standing around. Do not take his words lightly. The people furthest from the kingdom of God are those who seem most to have it in hand.

We Go Beyond Goodness To Grace

The world on beyond perfection is where we go beyond just saying "yes" to really understanding the meaning of the word "no", and it is a place where we go beyond the enticing pull of legalism to genuine liberty in our relationship with God.

I might sum it up like this: In the land on beyond perfection, we go beyond goodness to grace. To be a moral person usually means to be a good person. But life needs more from us than mere goodness.

Thomas Long told about the process of examining seminary students for ordination in a Presbyterian church in North Carolina. The students must pass an intense examination out in a church somewhere. The ministers from that region get to grill a student on any point of theology for as long as they wish, and sometimes the questioning lasts a long time.

Thomas Long said that one of his clergy colleagues who has served the same congregation for more than thirty years sits in silence throughout these ordeals. He never said a word, never asked a question, never demanded a clarification, until the very end.

Then, just when the examinations seem to have run its course, the questioners were getting tired, and the seminary graduate starts to think the ordeal is over, this gentleman stood. "Look out there," he said. He pointed to a large window at the side of their meeting hall. "Tell me when you see someone walking out there."

So the candidate sat there, neck craned, and looked for a while. "I see someone," he said.

"Do you know the person?" asked Long's friend.

"No, I don't."

Said the elderly gentleman, "Describe that person to me, theologically."

This sage of North Carolina claimed that one of two reasons is always given. When you sift through all the academic lingo and verbal padding, some seminary graduates say something like this: "There goes a sinner who's on his way to hell unless he repents and gives his life over to Christ."

The other answer goes something like this: "There goes a person who is a child of God. God loves that person so very much, and the best thing that can happen to him is to find out how good it is to love God in return."

"They're both right," said the elderly man behind the strange question. "That's what the scriptures and the church have always said. Still, as I've watched these fellows come and go over the years, the ones who answer my question the second way make better pastors. Mark my words!"

Do you believe it? If you do, then you probably have already peeked into the world of Jesus' wisdom, the world on beyond perfection. For when the roll is called up yonder, the grades on the report cards that make it won't be *A* for excellent, *B* for good, or even *C* for nice try.

The only grade that will make it will be *G* for grace.

Up The Ladder To Nowhere

A mother was proud of her sons. They were disciples of the Rabbi Jesus that everyone was talking about! Can you believe it?!

Like any good mother, she just wanted the best for her boys. What mother wouldn't? So she begged an audience with the great man. First she flattered him: "Sir, I can see you are going places!" Then she got down to business: "Thank you for taking my sons with you. They are good men, aren't they? I'm sure they will help you run things when you come to power. Just give them a chance, okay?"

What mother wouldn't do that for her sons? Your mother does that for you, doesn't she? Proud parents! Just like you and me!

And she was not wrong, was she? James and John were truly good young men! She had a right to be proud of them. They had a right to be proud of themselves! Best friends of Jesus! Part of the next generation of Jewish leaders! In on the ground floor of the great revolutionary movement that Jesus was sure to bring in!

Their mother was proud of them. And they were proud of themselves!

Healthy self-esteem, we call it. Good for a person. Builds character! Leadership material!

Are you proud?

Robert Louis Stevenson wrote a little poem about pride (*A Child's Garden of Verses in the public domain*):

> When I am grown to man's estate
> I shall be very proud and great,
> And tell the other girls and boys
> Not to meddle with my toys!

We probably all feel that way sometimes, especially when someone bigger or haughtier than us walks all over our toys or our self-esteem. Even though we feel like little people many times, we're much too proud to stay that way.

The opening sentences of Bonamy Dobree's famous biography of John Wesley capture his struggle with pride: "It is difficult to be humble. Even if you aim at humility, there is no guarantee that when you have attained the state you will not be proud of the feat." Isn't that the truth?

Pride is so subtle. In ancient Greece, the philosopher Diogenes came to Plato's house one day. He already felt that Plato was not as good a teacher as he, and now he had the proof. On the floor of Plato's house were several ornate carpets, obviously very exquisite and costly. To show his contempt for such a waste of money, Diogenes walked all over them and then wiped his feet in a show of contempt. "Thus do I trample upon the pride of Plato!" he said.

Plato observed quietly: "With even greater pride, it seems."

The Subtle Sin

"The proud hate pride—in others!" said Benjamin Franklin. And somehow our pointing fingers have to turn round to our own hearts. The disciples of Jesus were about to find this out when they argued about who deserved what positions of honor next to Jesus.

C. S. Lewis observed that "unchastity, anger, greed, drunkenness and all that are mere flea bites in comparison with pride."

So how do we come to the humility of Jesus? And how can we be sure that we aren't proud of our humility when we get there?

Perhaps it demands, first of all, that we take our eyes off ourselves. The truest way to be humble, as Phillips Brooks said, "is not to stoop until you are smaller than yourself, but to stand at your real height against some higher nature that will show you what the real smallness of your greatness is."

Many people in Jesus' day were worse than his disciples, morally, socially, and spiritually. But setting themselves up against others would do nothing to challenge the evil in their own hearts, nor put them on the road to a higher quality of life. Only a vision of God's glory can do that — and that is the strength of Jesus' own humility.

The only way to defeat pride is to make it irrelevant. Once, when conductor Arturo Toscanini was preparing an orchestra and chorus for a performance, he was forced to work with a rather temperamental soprano soloist. His every suggestion was turned aside by her haughty opinions.

At one point she loudly proclaimed: "I am the star of this performance!" Toscanini looked at her with quiet pity. "Madam," he said, "in this performance there are no stars. There is only the music."

In that moment her pride became irrelevant. It was swallowed up in the larger glory of the music. Personal arrogance was like a third left shoe. Who needs it?

So too with James and John. So too with us. As Isaac Watts put it in his well-known hymn:

> When I survey the wondrous cross
> On which the Prince of Glory died,
> My richest gain I count but loss,
> And pour contempt on all my pride. (public domain)

"Humph"s That Kill

Do you remember Rudyard Kipling's tale of "How the Camel Got Its Hump"? At the dawn of creation, according to Kipling, God gave each of his wonderful animals a job to do. Working together they began to prepare the new world for the coming of humankind.

The only one among them that would not work was the camel. Whenever the other animals asked for his help, he just said, "Humph!!" and walked away. The camel, according to Kipling, thought he was better than all the other animals, so he "Humph!!"ed around every day with his proud nose in the air, and a disdainful swagger in his legs.

But when God saw what was happening, he collected all of the haughty camel's "Humph!!"s, and one day dumped them right down onto the camel's back. And that, said Kipling, is how the camel got its hump.

Proud people a lot like camels, aren't they? Noses in the air, swaggering steps, and humps of self-importance pushing up wherever they invade the company of others. Mid-twentieth-century Italian dictator Benito Mussolini played the part so well. Although he was short of stature, he was long on pride. People used to say that he could strut even when he was sitting down. A newspaper once reported that "He was a solemn procession of one."

Self-Absorbed

Pride is a funny thing. It is an extension of many very good qualities that God has given us as gifts. Why, then, does a great athlete cross the line from confidence to cockiness? What pushes a beautiful woman from graciousness to arrogance? When does a businessman step up one rung too high on the ladder of success and become self-important? How can disciples of Jesus claim positions of honor in his kingdom?

The ancient Greeks tried to define the transition from piety to pride in the story of Narcissus. Narcissus was a wonderfully beautiful young man, greatly talented and admired. Unfortunately, he had ears large enough to hear the whispers of appreciation that buzzed through every crowd when he approached. Soon he began to believe what others said, and then fell in love with himself.

One the day he was scrambling through the rocks of the hills on a hunt. Thirsty, he paused at a pool in the hollows, and bent down to drink. But before his lips broke the mirrored surface, he caught sight of a marvelous water nymph staring at him from below. He was entranced by the beautiful face, the wonderful eyes, the marvelous nose and chin, and reached down to embrace the nymph.

Yet when he disturbed the water it seemed as if the nymph scurried away. That pained him deeply and he began to cry. When the ripples subsided, the nymph was back. Though Narcissus didn't seem to catch on, he was actually seeing himself.

Over and over the scene repeated itself—Narcissus staring in love at his own reflection in the pool—until he finally fell famished to his death!

The point was clear: the moment we begin to love ourselves as the highest good we lose the power to live authentically. We cross the line from piety to pride when we become the object of our own appreciation.

This is a perplexing issue, however, since we all need self-esteem to function to our fullest potential. The concern Jesus had with James and John in today's gospel lesson becomes a matter of where that self-esteem originates. When we are loved by another, our self-esteem grows. The source of the power is located outside of ourselves and energizes us to be the best we can be. Once we fall in love with ourselves, the empowerment becomes cancerous, and we destroy the very qualities that might otherwise make us lovely.

Tony Campolo said it well. When he was in seminary, taking his first class in preaching, he was already a very gifted speaker. After his first "practice" sermon to his fellow-students and professor, his peers praised him up one side and down the other. He couldn't wait to see what his professor wrote.

The evaluation came back with a single line in red marking ink: "Tony, you can't convince people that you're wonderful and that Jesus is wonderful in the same sermon."

That is why Jesus needed to put his disciples all in their places. They could not love anyone else when they were obsessed with themselves, even if their obsession was for holy living or righteous behavior.

What Kind Of People Are We?

Our lives reflect the struggles of choices made and often choices regretted. Think of Corrie ten Boom, who tells her story in *The Hiding Place*. During World War II, her family hid some Jews to keep them from the gas chambers. She and her father needed to find a safe place for one Jewish mother and her very young child.

One day a local clergyman stepped into their watch shop. They decided to ask him if he would take these two frightened ones into his home. He refused, however. Corrie couldn't believe it at the time, so she impulsively ran to the mother and grabbed the little baby from her arms. She brought the child to the pastor and tried to thrust him into the pastor's hands.

Again he refused. "No!" he said. "Definitely not! We could lose our lives for that Jewish child."

Who could blame him? How could he help others, if he himself were dragged away to the concentration camps? That was his decision as he wrestled with himself in the gray area of his circumstances.

Father ten Boom gathered the little one in his arm and said to the pastor, "You say we could lose our lives for this child. I would consider that the greatest honor that could come to my family." Another self. Another choice. You and I wrestle with such choices every day of our lives.

Think of the things we say:

- *"I don't really feel like myself today."*
- *"I'm so ashamed of myself!"*
- *"For a moment there I forgot myself."*
- *"I just hate myself!"*

What are we saying? What is really happening to us?

We think we are making our way in life. We think we know the self that is best for us. We think we can find a way to swim outside of the ocean, a way to fly without looking up to the heavens or to grow without digging deep. But we can't, can we? We cannot, until love wrestles us in the night and gives us a new name. For in the end, God must wrestle with us as he did with Jacob many generations before. God must wrestle with us, or the choices of our hearts will lead us astray.

Proper 25 / Ordinary Time 30
Mark 10:46-52

"I Want to See"

In Morris West's novel *The Clowns of God*, there's a powerful scene where a father and his daughter were having an argument. She told him that she was going to go to Paris to live with her boyfriend. He wouldn't let her. Why would she want to do something like that?

Because I'm afraid, she said.

Afraid? Whatever are you afraid of?

She said: I'm "afraid of getting married and having children and trying to make a home, while the whole world could tumble round our ears in a day." She went on: "You older ones don't understand. You've survived a war. You've built things. You've raised families... But look at the world you've left to us! You've given us everything except tomorrow."

"Everything except tomorrow." And tomorrow is the one thing that we need the most.

No Horizon

One newspaper recently carried this ad in its classified section: *Hope chest—brand-new. Half price. Long story.*

We have had so many long stories in our lives. We have had so many broken promises. And we have had so many shattered dreams. We're ready to give up. No more promises. No more commitments. Everything except tomorrow.

That is the situation with blind Bartimaeus on the road from Jericho to Jerusalem. He is a capable person with limited horizons. The light of definition is gone. Within his head, the world and the universe function perfectly, but extending these into daily life is difficulty because of his inability to see others and things around him.

Though most of us have the capability of physical sight, we are too often limited with him. We live in a trembling world. We face an uncertain future. We are surrounded by a host of plagues and troubles. We cannot see the way ahead.

Still, in the middle of it all stands Jesus, on the road with us. The old hymn puts it this way:

> Thou didst reach forth Thy hand and mine enfold;
> I walked and sank not on the storm-vexed sea!
> 'Twas not so much that I on Thee took hold,
> As Thou, dear Lord, on me, on me. (public domain)

Donna Hoffman, a young Christian mother who battled cancer for a number of years, wrote this little poem in her journal. She was in the hospital at the time. The cancer seemed so strong, and tomorrow seemed like an uncertain dream or a tragic nightmare. She called her poem "Journey":

> My soul runs arms outstretched down the corridor to you.
> Ah, my feet may stumble but how my heart can stride!

That was the testimony of Bartimaeus when he called out to Jesus. It is our cry as well. Only God's grace can sustain us in a world turned upside down, even when our feet stumble, even when the journey seems too long, too troublesome, even when we cannot see the way ahead. "My soul runs. How my heart can stride!"

Generations ago, young William Borden went to Yale University. He was the wealthy son of a powerful family. He could do anything in life that he chose. When he graduated, he chose to become a missionary of the gospel of Jesus Christ.

His friends thought he was crazy. "Why throw your life away like that?" they said. "You have so much to live for here."

But Borden knew who held his tomorrows. He made his choices. And God gave him the inner strength to live his convictions.

He set out on a long journey to China. It took months in those days. By the time he got to Egypt, some disease managed to make him sick. He was placed in a hospital. Soon it became obvious that he wouldn't recover. William Borden would die a foreigner in Egypt. He never reached his goal. He never went back home.

He could have been troubled by the tragedy of it all. But his last conscious act was to write a little note. Seven words. Seven words that they spoke at his funeral. Seven words that summarized his life, his identity: "No reserve, no retreat, and no regrets!"

Can you say that? Those who spend time on the road with Bartimaeus, those who see with the eyes of faith, those who travel with Jesus toward Jerusalem can.

Famous psychiatrist Viktor Frankl remembered powerfully a day of despair turned to hope during World War II. Frankl was on a work gang, just outside the fences that hid the horrors of Hitler's infamous death camp at Dachau. "We were at work in a trench," wrote Frankl. "The dawn was gray around us; gray was the sky above; gray the snow in the pale light of dawn; gray rags in which my fellow prisoners were clad, and gray their faces."

Frankl told how he was ready to die. It was as if the gray bleakness had claws, and each moment they dug deeper and colder into his soul. Why go on? What could be the purpose in "living" if, indeed, he was even still alive at this moment? There was no heaven, no hell, no future, no past. Only the clutching grayness of this miserable moment. He was at one with hopeless depressed.

Suddenly, to his surprise, Frankl felt "a last violent protest" surging within himself. He sensed that even though his body had given up and his mind had accepted defeat, his inner spirit was taking flight. It was searching. It was looking. It was scanning the eternal horizons for the faintest glimmer that said his fleeting life had some divine purpose. It was looking for God.

In a single instant two things happened, said Frankl, that simply could not be mere coincidence. Within, he heard a powerful cry, piercing the gloom and tearing at the icy claws of death. The voice shouted "yes!" against the "no" of defeat and the gray "I don't know" of the moment.

At that exact second, "a light was lit in a distant farmhouse." Like a beacon it called attention to itself. It spoke of life and warmth and family and love. Frankl said that in that moment he began to believe, and in that moment he began to live again.

We often have the same need. The grayness of bleak days is stifling. The loneliness of the moment overwhelms. The blindness of our limitations and uncertainties keeps us frozen and falling. Is there a reason to carry on? Is there meaning beyond the drudgery of today's repetitive struggles? Is there hope and is there God?

"Send forth your light and your truth," we shout with the psalmist (43:3). Don't leave me alone! Give me some sign! Light a candle in the window and take me home!

John Greenleaf Whittier put it this way:

> A tender child of summers three,
> Seeking her little bed at night,
> Paused on the dark stair timidly,
> "O Mother! take my hand," said she,
> "And then the dark will all be light."
>
> We older children grope our way,
> From dark behind to dark before:
> And only when our hands we lay,
> Dear Lord, in Thine, the night is day,
> And there is darkness nevermore.
>
> Reach downward to the sunless days,
> Wherein our guides are blind as we,
> And faith is small and hope delays:
> Take Thou the hands of prayer we raise,
> And let us feel the light of Thee. (public domain)

Bartimaeus' story mixed despair with hope, for God never denies us the light we need. As Joyce Kilmer wrote:

> Because the way was steep and long, and through a strange and lonely land,
> God placed upon my lips a song and put a lantern in my hand.
> And suddenly we know the way home. (public domain)

Navigation Assist

One man told of sitting next to a passenger taking his first flight. The novice was obviously ill at ease: squirming in his seat, looking out the window to see if the wings were still there, gripping the armrests in a knuckle lock. Every little bump or jolt would bring a gasp and a prayer, and one hand nervously fingering a rosary bead.

The experienced traveler grinned a bit, and thought he might calm his seat-mate's nerves with some religious psychology. "What are you so worried about?" he asked. "You're a religious person! Didn't Jesus say, in the Bible, 'I am with you always, even to the ends of the earth?!'"

"No!" his partner fairly shouted. "You've got it wrong! Jesus said, '*Lo*, I am with you always!' I'm not sure what happens when you get way up here!"

Where Are We Going?
High or low, worry is part of human life. Jesus understood that. In fact, the Bible seems to indicate that Jesus worried at times right along with the rest of us. In John 12, for instance, we read of Jesus' entry into Jerusalem at the start of the week that would bring his death. The crowds surrounded him, and he was well aware of the troubles that would come in the next few days. When he arrived at the temple square to pray, he shouted a note of worry to the skies. "Now my heart is troubled!" he said. The word he used, as it comes to us in the Greek text, is one that echoes our fears. It means agitated, unsettled, anxious, frightened, or disturbed.

Jesus sounded like one of us, didn't he? He worried too! And that is why he understood this "teacher of the law" who approached him from the crowd. The man's question seems theological to us, and not very worrisome. But in Jesus' day, the whole context shows how worried this man was. He was a "teacher of the law"! People came to him for guidance. They asked him about the morality of little things, simple actions day by day. He always had an answer. He was a "teacher of the law," after all! He was trained for this!

Yet when he heard Jesus speak, the man's theology began to seem stilted and cold, perhaps even irrelevant. Jesus talked about things as if he knew both God and life. Jesus connected the dots.

The man became confused. All his philosophic reflection and intricate ethical stasis came off as trite. His answers did not seem very helpful or convincing. Was his devotion misplaced? Had he mistaken his vocation? Was he not really a "teacher of the law"? He was worried.

But worry is a part of human life. Do you know anyone who never worries? Only a machine cannot worry! Only a robot never gets anxious!

Erma Bombeck once wrote about the fears of a young fellow on the way to his first day at school: "My name is Donald, and I don't know anything! I have new underwear, a new sweater, a loose tooth, and I didn't sleep well last night; I worried. What if the school bus jerks after I get on, and I lose my balance and my pants rip and everyone laughs? What if a bell rings and a man yells, "Where do you belong?" and I don't know? What if the thermos lid on my soup is on too tight and when I try to open it, it breaks? What if I splash water on my name tag and my name disappears and no one will know who I am? What if they send us out to play and all the swings are taken?"

Though she wrote about a child, Erma Bombeck took our everyday fears and echoed them through the mind of a six-year-old.

We all worry. It's part of life. G. K. Chesterton was once asked by a reporter, "If you were a preacher and you had only one sermon to give, what would it be about?"

Chesterton didn't think twice. He said, "I'd preach about worry!" He knew what it was to be human. Worry is a part of life, and something that drives a lot of our actions. Jesus knew that as he quietly paused pastorally with this worried man.

We Worry About Things That Matter To Us
We worry about the things that are close to us, the things that are constantly with us, the things that we carrying around with us day after day. We worry about the things that have the most immediate value to us.

Maybe that is really the point of why Jesus turned the man's question back on himself. His worries were essentially the test of his values. We worry about things that are the most important to us in life.

In essence, Jesus encouraged the "teacher of the law, and we with him, to take the "Worry Test." What are you most anxious about? What troubles you the most? What keeps you awake at night, or disturbs your thoughts most often during the day?

When we take the test we find out where our hearts are. The worry test teaches us the schedule of values in our lives.

It is like the story someone told of two men on a cross-country bike trip. They were traveling together on a tandem bike. For the first short while the land was level, and they pumped along with energy and style, enjoying this teamwork. But then the horizon began to rise, and they found themselves fighting a steep climb. Panting and puffing they slowly worked their way to the top.

Finally, they reached the summit, and stopped to catch their breaths. "Whew!" said one, wiping the sweat off his face, "that was some hard climb!"

"Yeah!" said the other, "and if I hadn't kept the brake on we probably would have slid back to the bottom!"

That's the "Worry Test" in action, isn't it? The one fellow had his mind on the heights. He was going to make it to the top if it took all of his energies and strength. Meanwhile his partner has his mind on the bottom. He was worried about sliding back, about being sucked down the hill. They are both doing the same thing, riding the same bike on the same road up the same hill, but their values are at different places. Their worries set them apart.

We can see the "teacher of the law," can't we? He was worried. His eyes were down. He feared that he would be caught as a fraud. What if, after all his study, after gaining a reputation, there was nothing behind the paper?! What if he was only a shell of projection? What if, after he had pretended to guide others, he could not find the way himself? What if God graded him with an "F"?

So it is with us. We all worry, said Jesus, but our worries surround the things that we value most in life. Take the "Worry Test," he told us. List the concerns that bother you the most. When you read your list over, you'll find your heart! In another place, Jesus put it like this: "For where your treasure is, there your heart will be also." (Matthew 6:21)

What Do We Worry About?

The challenge of Jesus is not to stop worrying altogether. To be human is to have worries, frets, and cares. We are affected by life. The issue, according to Jesus, is to change our goals and values and treasure so that, in the end, our worries will take on a more godly character. "What do you think," said Jesus to the man. In essence, he was redirecting the man's own question back into his heart "What is your focus? What are you concerned about?"

Alexander Solzenitsyn remembered how it came to him during his days in the Siberian labor camps. He had lost his family. His days stretched out in endless backbreaking efforts. Then the doctors told him he had cancer. There was no cure. He would die soon.

The next day, he said, he barely got out of his bunk. His heart was gone. His mind was numb. He had no energy as he left to join the others in the dawn work patrol. "What's the use?" he asked himself.

Solzenitsyn said that when he got to the rock quarries he dropped his shovel, sat down, resting his head on his tired, folded arms. He knew the guards would see him soon, but he didn't care. He hoped that they would shoot him. Then, at least, the pain would be over and the worries gone.

"Just then," he wrote, "I felt someone standing near me. I looked up, and there was an old man. I'd never seen him before. I don't remember ever seeing him again. But he knelt over me, he took a stick, and he drew a cross on the ground in front of me."

That little act of a stranger did something for Solzenitsyn. "That cross," he said, "made me see things in a new way! There's a power in this universe that is bigger than any empire or any government! There's a God who experiences our pain and who dies our death and who came back from the tombs. There's a God who gives life meaning, who is LIFE itself! That's what really matters here! That's why we exist! That's why Jesus came to earth for us!"

Solzenitsyn said that he sat there thinking about it all for a few more minutes. Then he stood up, picked up his shovel, and went back to work. Things wouldn't change around him for over a year, but inside he was a new person. God lives! God cares! God is working out his purposes!

That put Solzenitsyn's worries in their place. They didn't vanish or disappear suddenly. Instead, they were caught up into a larger perspective of concern. How can I share the life of the Master?! How can my days be a reflection of his kingdom, his power, and his glory? That is why Jesus affirmed the man, as he walked away, thoughtfully. When he had to face his own inner self, he knew what mattered most. He loved God. And even when he didn't love God fully or truly, he wanted to love God. That was his highest value. He loved others. Even when he was selfish and self-absorbed, his heart kept calling out for him to see those around him and honor them and care about them. In the actions of his daily life, this "teacher of the Law" was a child of God and a neighbor to others.

That is where Jesus is leading his disciples as well, and us along with them. "You are not far from the kingdom of God," he said to the man. Do you see him glancing at you also?

That is a hard lesson to learn. We are so good at taking control of our lives. We are very good at trying to play God, to the point that we don't want him to remind us of the real structures of life.

Some years ago, when Dick Shepard was the vicar of an Anglican parish in London, England, he had a very vivid dream. It stayed with him after he woke. His life was exceptionally busy in those days, constantly trying to meet the demands of the many people under his care in ministry.

One day he felt himself coming down with the flu. But he knew that he could not afford to get sick! He did not have the time! There were too many things to do! There were sermons to write, and classes to prepare, and meetings to chair, and people to visit! His congregation needed him! His family needed him! Even God needed him! He just could not afford to get sick right now!

That night he had his terrible nightmare. He dreamed that he was standing in heaven near to God's throne. An angelic telegram arrived, and the messenger handed the envelope to God. God tore it open and read these horrifying words: "Dick Shepard is about to be ill."

Then, said Reverend Shepard, God began to wring his hands. A worried look clouded God's face, and God began to mumble to the angels: "Oh, no! Dick Shepard is about to be ill! Whatever shall we do? Whatever shall I do?"

When Pastor Shepard woke up in the morning he had a good laugh. He decided that God could probably manage somehow without him, and he stopped living as if all the world depended on him.

That is the lesson that Jesus wanted his disciples to learn from this brief encounter. Only that lesson will change our values and redefine our goals, and point us toward new treasures as well. "Love God first. Love your neighbor." That is enough.

What Is Our Goal?

Fred Craddock reminded us of that in a story he passed along about a sermon of his that took on a life of its own. He had titled the sermon "Doxology," and he had preached it a number of times — enough so that it gained quite a reputation among his family and friends. The message of "Doxology" was all about the meaning of life and the reason why we exist. It said that the ultimate goal of our time on earth is to bring glory to God, no matter what the circumstances. Fred said that that sermon led to one of the most beautiful experiences of his life.

"I was on the phone," he wrote. "My oldest brother had just died. Heart attack. When stunned and hurt, get real busy to avoid thought.

"Call the wife. Get the kids out of school. Arrange for a colleague to take my classes. Cancel a speaking engagement.

"And, oh yes, stop the milk, the paper, the mail; have someone feed the dog...

"All night we drove, across two states, eyes pasted against the windshield. Conversation was spasmodic, consisting of taking turns asking the same question over and over.

"When we drew near the town and the house, I searched my mind for a word to speak to the widow. He was my brother, but he was her husband. I was still searching when we pulled into the driveway. She came out to meet us and as I opened the car door, still without that word, she broke the silence: 'I hope you brought *Doxology*!'

"*Doxology?*" wrote Fred. "No, I hadn't even thought of [that sermon] since the phone call. But the truth is now clear: if we ever lose our Doxology, we might as well be dead."

Isn't that true? We will never stop worrying. We will never still our anxious hearts. But when we take the "Worry Test," and when we find out where our treasures really lie, and when we learn to sing the *Doxology* in all circumstance of life, then Jesus' words will have come home in us!

Public Piety?

When I was a college student, our president was a person who always said what was on his mind. He had a very healthy self-image, and he was not concerned about how others might respond. At one graduation ceremony he stood at the podium and looked out over the huge crowd of people. He shook his head and said to himself (right into the microphone, of course!): "All these Christians in one place, and no one's taking an offering!"

We take offerings a lot, don't we? Every Sunday when you come to worship, the money plates are passed. In fact, you can hardly think of a meeting of Christians where there isn't some suggestion about offerings, donations, or contributions. Money and religion seem to go hand in hand these days.

Indeed, someone told the story of an airplane experiencing problems. One of the engines had failed, and another was acting strange. The passengers were getting nervous. Some were beginning to panic. Finally, one fellow sitting near the front of the plane yelled out, "Is there a priest of a minister on board who can do something religious?" So, yes, a clergyman got up, and passed his hat for an offering!

Money and religion often go hand in hand! But maybe they should. They certainly did for Jesus. The gospels record 37 of his parables, and in nearly *half* of them - *sixteen*, to be exact — Jesus talked about money and the way in which we use our possessions!

More than that: one-tenth of all the verses in the gospels deal directly with the subject of money! That's 288 verses! Again, when you look at the whole Bible, you find that less than 500 verses speak specifically about faith, and only 500 verses talk about prayer, yet more than 2,000 verses address the topics of money and possessions!

Religion and money go hand in hand. That is essentially what Jesus was saying in these verses: "Your money and your religion go hand in hand! Your faith and your finances are part of the same package! What you do with your checkbook is as important as what you do with your Bible!" Religion and money go hand in hand.

In that light there are three questions we have to face.

Are You Aware?

The first is this: "Are you aware?" Do you see others around you? Has your faith opened your eyes to the need and the concerns of your partners in the human race?

Probably no period in human history was as peaceful and as prosperous as the days of Antonius Pious (138-161 AD), who ruled Rome in the second century. Edward Gibbon, in his magnificent treatise *The Decline and Fall of the Roman Empire*, said that the times of Antonius Pious were the "happiest" on earth! He was probably right. There was more wealth and business success and domestic peace in those days than most civilizations have ever known.

Antonius Pious was a good ruler, and his people knew it. In fact, one of his biggest supporters was the Athenian philosopher Aristedes. Aristedes could not seem to write enough verses in praise of Antonius. He lauded the government, and the beauty of Rome. He praised the magnificence of its buildings and the character of its citizens. Aristedes was a one-man ministry of propaganda, telling the world of the pomp and splendor of Antonius Pious and his great government.

But Aristedes wrote about other things as well. One day he sent a letter to Antonius, telling the monarch to keep his eye on a certain group of people in his empire. "You need these people," said Aristedes. "You should find them and talk with them. You can learn much from them."

The unique thing about them, said Aristedes, is that they really had eyes to see others. They watched out for those around them. They took care of the widows, who were often pushed aside when their husbands died. They looked after orphans, especially those who got sold as slaves. Those people would even pay huge sums of money to buy the freedom of others.

It was not that these folks were so wealthy. In fact, said Aristedes, they were often the very poor of most Roman cities. Yet if they knew of someone in need, they would even go without food for two or three days in order to save a few coins that might help someone else.

"You should get to know these people, Antonius!" said Aristedes. "In all your grand empire they are the only ones who make it a habit to see the needs of the poor and do something about it."

Who was Aristedes writing about? Christians! He was writing about the followers of Jesus! Can you imagine it? A Greek philosopher told one of the greatest Roman emperors to look for Christians because they were the ones from whom he could learn something!

That is why Jesus asked us this morning, "Are you aware?" Do you see? Have you reached beyond yourself and looked at the lives and the circumstances of your partners in the human enterprise?

One of the greatest statements about Jesus comes in a story that is told by all four of the gospel writers. Jesus had had a busy day. People demanded a lot of him. He was tired from traveling around and talking with the crowds. His power had been drained by the many sick who came to him begging to be healed.

Now it was late. The disciples wanted to send the crowds away. They should go home, and Jesus needed to find a place to rest for the night. But the gospel writers told us that Jesus looked at the people around him and he had *compassion* on them, and then he gave them food and rest.

He looked.

He saw.

He felt.

He touched.

That is our Lord! That is the character of Jesus! And today he says to us: "Are you aware?" Do you see the needs of those around you? Can you feel the hurts that are throbbing through your world? Are you aware?

In 1966, evangelist Martin Higgenbottem was one of the main speakers at the Berlin World Congress on Evangelism. He told the gathering that his life of devotion and service had to do with his mother. He remembered coming home from school one afternoon to find her sitting at the kitchen table with a strange man. The fellow was obviously someone who lived on the streets. His clothes were filthy, his hair was slicked with unwashed grease, his body smelled of a mixture of unkind odors.

But Martin's mother was chatting pleasantly with him while they devoured a plate of sandwiches together. She had gone shopping that morning and found him cold and hungry, so she brought him home with her.

When the man was ready to leave he said passionately, "I wish there were more people in the world like you!"

Martin's mother casually threw the compliment aside. "Oh," she said, "there are! You just have to look for them!"

The man broke down. He shook his head, and tears rolled across his cheeks. "But lady!" he said, "I didn't have to look for you! You looked for me!"

You looked for me!

"Are you aware?" asked Jesus. Not like pious folks who parade their good deeds and great contributions as if they are an end in themselves. Do you actually see others and their needs? Are you aware?

Will You Share?

A second question follows: "Will you share?" Will you take what you have and give to those around you? Will you use your blessings to touch the lives of others?

There is a wonderful story told about Fiorello La Guardia. He was mayor of New York City during the Great Depression, and today one of the city's airports is named after him.

Before he became mayor he served for a time as a police court judge. One cold winter's day they brought a man to him who was charged with stealing a loaf of bread. La Guardia asked him if he was guilty. The man nodded. He had taken the bread because his family was starving, and he had no money to buy food. What was he to do?

The law bound La Guardia. "I've got to punish you," he told the man. "The law makes no exceptions! I fine you $10!" And he brought down his gavel.

But where would the man get the money for the fine? They would have to throw him in jail as well!

La Guardia was not finished, though. He already had his hand on his wallet. He pulled out a ten-dollar bill, handed it to the bailiff and said: "Here's the money for your fine."

Then he took back the ten dollar bill, put it into his hat, handed the hat to the bailiff and said, "I'm going to suspend the sentence, and I'm going to fine everyone here in the courtroom fifty cents for living in a town where a man has to steal bread in order to eat!"

When the man left the courtroom that day he had the light of life in his eyes, and 47 dollars and fifty cents in his pocket!

"Will you share?" Will you share what God has given you with others around who have needs today?

It was a requirement of the Jewish religion to give alms for the poor. That is what Jesus is talking about in these verses. In fact, the Old Testament rules and regulations had a built-in system that guaranteed help for the poor. You were not even allowed to come to the temple for worship unless you had given alms to the poor. So these folks, whatever their status in society, all brought coins to the temple as they came to worship. It was a public show of religious commitment and shared community solidarity.

Tithing was a standard practice. One tenth of everything you ever earned was to be given back to God as a confession of faith. But how can you give money to God? Do the deacons take the offerings and go into the back room of the church and toss it all up to heaven, and whatever God does not want falls back to the floor?

No, God's instructions were very clear. When you give your tithes to the poor, he said, you are giving them to me! Jesus echoed that idea in Matthew 25, when he talked about the end of time, and the day we will all appear before the throne of God for judgment. God will say to some of us: "You took care of me! When I was hungry, you fed me. When I was naked, you clothed me. When I was sick, you looked after me."

We will shake our heads, said Jesus, and have this puzzled look on our faces. We will say to God: "When was that? I don't remember ever seeing you on earth! When did we help you out like that?"

The Father will look at us, said Jesus, and he will say: "When you gave to the poor among you, when you offered help to those who needed it, when you went beyond yourself in mercy, you did it to me!"

We do not always do well at that, do we? The Internal Revenue Service tells us that few of us even admit to giving for charitable causes. Americans give only about 1.65% of their incomes to charity! That includes *all* charitable causes, like the arts, universities, hospitals, and cultural centers! That is 85% *less* than tithing! And even of that figure, only a small portion of the money actually goes to poor people!

It is not that we are isolated from the needs in our world. We hear the news, we see the pictures, we're challenged by the requests that come every day in the mail. When Jesus asked us, "Are you aware?" we can only say, "Yes! Painfully so! Enormously so!"

But when Jesus asked us, "Will you share?" that was a different story. We are programmed to take, rather than give. We are taught by our society to receive, but not necessarily to share. We are challenged by our age to grab for all the gusto we can get, and not to deprive ourselves of anything for the sake of others.

John Bright, a British politician of the nineteenth century, was walking down a street one day when a fellow was seriously injured in an accident. The crowds gathered around, gasping in delighted horror at the blood and the gore. But Bright took off his hat, grabbed a ten-pound note from his wallet, and stuffed it into his hat. Then he pushed his way through the crowds and said, "I'm ten pounds sorry for this man! How sorry are you?!"

In moments he had turned the sickening curiosity of the people into sympathetic compassion.

Are you aware?

Will you share?

Those are the questions of Jesus for us.

Do You Care?

Then came the most important question of all. "Do you care?"

Do you really care about others? Is compassion a way of life for you?

Helmut Thielicke told of a time he was hospitalized in great pain. The nurses were wonderful, and took great care of him. One nurse, in particular, impressed him. She worked the night shift. Every evening she was there: prompt, pleasant, and efficient. She seemed to care deeply about her patients. She always had a bright smile for them.

In fact, in the sleepless hours of the night she often sat next to Thielicke and talked with him. For twenty years she had been on this shift! For twenty years, she had worked while others slept! She had given of herself in the darkest hours of the night.

"Isn't it a pretty stressful thing for you?" Thielicke asked her. "Don't you ever get tired of it all? How do you keep it up, year after year?"

She beamed at me, Thielicke said, and this is what she told me: "Well, you see, every night that I work sets another jewel in my heavenly crown! I've already got 7,175 in a row!"

Thielicke said he was stunned! Suddenly his gratitude toward her was gone. She didn't really care about him! She wasn't helping him through his tough times because she felt compassion for him! She was only doing this in order to earn some kind of reward! Every night she kept count of her good deeds! Every smile was sold at a price! Every shift was a deposit in the bank of heaven, and that's all!

Sure, she was aware! Yes, she was willing to share! But did she care? Did her heart go with the gift? Did her spirit reach with her fingers and touch the one she tended? When she told the reason for her service it seemed not.

Jesus talked in these verses about the rewards we get from God for the gifts of charity we give during our lives. Yet there is something crass and dirty when the rewards become our goals.

Some years ago, a man in Florida brought a lawsuit against his church. He demanded that the church return to him the $800 that he had given to it the year before. His court documents included this testimony: *"On September 7 I delivered $800 of my savings to the (X) church in response to the pastor's promise that blessings, benefits, and reward would come to the person who tithed his wealth. I did not and have not received these benefits."*

You foolish man! Jesus would have said. You silly beggar! Do you give in order to get?! Do you tithe to earn a profit? Do you offer your services on the floor of the trading markets?! Said one writer: "He that serves God for money will serve the devil for better wages!" (Sir Roger L'Estrange)

He is right! That was exactly Jesus' point. "Are you aware?" he asked us. "Yes!" we tell him. We see the needs around us.

"Will you share?" he requested of us. "Well, that's tough for us," we answer, "but we'll try."

Then comes the hard part. "But do you care?" Do you reach yourself with the gift? Do you touch the heart of the needy, and feel his hurts, know her wounds, and stretch your hand in love and compassion? Do you care?

So often we don't even hear his question. We are too busy asking a question ourselves: *What's in it for me? What do I get out of it? Will anybody notice? Do I get the "Good Citizen of the Year" award? Will there be a write-up in the papers?*

One man I know served in the church all his life. In his senior years, however, he became bitter. Nobody had ever really thanked him! None of the younger people in the church realized how much he had given! So he pulled back and wrapped himself in a security blanket of self-pity.

One woman's face was wet with tears when she came to see me. All these years she had volunteered her time and talents! Other women went out and got jobs, and earned money. But she always felt it was her responsibility to visit the needy, to make meals for the poor, and to call on the sick at the hospital every week. Now she was tired of it all. Nobody cared what she had done! Nobody had ever stood up and thanked her publicly! Why should she give any more of herself if people were so ungracious?

"Why indeed?" asked Jesus. If that is what it is all about, why indeed?

In his sermon "The Weight of Glory," C. S. Lewis talked about the idea of rewards in the Christian faith. Yes, he said, God promises us a reward for what we do in his name. But that does not make us mercenaries, giving in order to get, selling our good deeds on the open market.

If a man would marry a woman with great wealth in order to get her money for himself, said Lewis, we would call him mercenary, and rightly so. We would thumb our noses at him, and be appalled at his audacity.

But if a man married a rich woman only because he expected the reward of love, said Lewis, we would think him the greatest fellow on earth. He would be getting his reward, but it would actually be the fulfillment of what he is himself giving to the other! His reward was the extension of his gift.

So it is with us, says Lewis. We give of ourselves in Christian charity. We give of our time, our talents, our money. And, as Jesus said, God will reward us.

But what will that reward be? A million dollars? A life without sickness or cancer? A public declaration of our good deeds?

No.

The reward is simply to become one with *love* itself, to give as we have been given, to share in the delights of his sharing, to stretch our souls and to find ourselves.

"I think," said Annie Dillard, "that the dying prayer at last is not 'please,' but 'thank you,' as a guest thanks his host at the door."

She is right. Life on earth is not about a demand for recognition, but a quiet "thank-you" for all that we have been able to see and show and share.

That does not necessarily make good copy in the morning newspaper. Nor does it inevitably mean that we will be "successful" in life, at least in the ways many count success.

King Oswin, an early ruler of a northern territory in Britain, once gave his prize stallion to the local bishop as a token of appreciation. As the bishop traveled, he met a beggar along the road. Since the man had nothing at all, the bishop got off his fine steed and put the reigns in the man's hand. "Take him!" ordered the bishop. "Sell him and live! He's all I have to give you."

When King Oswin found out what the bishop had done he said, "Why didn't you send him to me? We have dozens of old horses that are more fitting for a beggar!"

The bishop quietly asked, "Is that stallion worth more than a child of God?!"

King Oswin thought about the question for a moment, and suddenly threw off his royal robes, falling at the bishop's feet and crying to God for forgiveness. The bishop blessed him and sent him away in peace. But for a long time he stared after the king with sorrowful eyes. When one asked him why he was so troubled, bishop Adrian replied: "I know that the king will not live long, for I have never seen a king so humble as he is. He will be taken from us, as the country is not worthy to have such a king."

His words proved true. In 651, the king was murdered by a neighboring rival who used Oswin's own kindness to gain an audience — and the world was poorer that day.

But you are still here, and I am still here. And today we have heard again the questions of Jesus.

"Are you aware?" Do you see the needs of others around you? Are your eyes open to the plight of the poor and the troubles of the destitute? Are you aware?

"Will you share?" Will you take whatever God has given you, and put it at the disposal of others? Will you see your goods and property as a loan on deposit from God to be shared in his name as others call for it? Will you share?

"Do you care?" That most of all. Ralph Waldo Emerson said: "Rings and jewels are not gifts, but apologies for gifts. The only gift is a portion of thyself." Is that the gift you give? Do you care? Does your heart stretch out with the love of Jesus? Does compassion flow in your veins? Have you found his reward in the act of love?

Chaos

"Why don't you believe in Jesus?"

I cringed as my student challenged our classroom guest. He was the distinguished head of the regional Chabad House, a deeply devout and highly respected Jewish rabbi. Everything about him oozed spirituality, from his black suit with the fringes of his prayer shawl peaking from under the coat, to his Moses-like white beard, to the shofar he blew at the beginning of class, announcing Rosh Hashanah.

We had tried to prepare our young scholars in the art of asking good questions without embarrassing our visitor. While reading Chiam Potok's powerful novel *My Name is Asher Lev* for our First Year Seminar on cultural diversity, we had arranged for the good rabbi to come. He knew Potok and had taught this book in other settings. As a representative of the conservative Jewish community, he understood well the world that Potok sought to portray.

My student wielded her weapon of words against the man, believing that she could demand that he recognize the superiority of her updated version of his ancient religion. The class tensed, knowing that worlds were colliding.

He sighed. Not in capitulation or exasperation, but almost in gentle pastoral resignation, knowing that his next words could prick the bubble of her carefully constructed theological presuppositions.

"You trust the Bible, don't you?" he asked, not specifying which Testament. Her head nodded, as did most in the room. "You believe what the prophets said about Messiah, right?" More affirmations.

"Well," he went on, "when I read the prophets, they tell me that when Messiah comes, wars will end, and people will no longer get sick, and there will be no famine or earthquakes. Everyone will live in peace and prosper."

He paused.

"Is that true of our world?" he asked.

Another weighty pause.

"You ask me why I don't believe in Jesus," he went on. "I do believe in Jesus. I am quite sure that Jesus was a good Jewish man who did many fine things for those around him in his day. But if I read the scriptures, the same ones that you read, then it is impossible for me to think that Jesus was the Messiah. The Bible itself keeps me from believing that."

He went on, soliciting other questions about Judaism and the practices of conservative believers in his world, and that of Potok and Asher Lev.

Is Jesus The Messiah?

My mind went on too. I could not help but admire the simple beauty of his logic and conclusions. My Christian teachings had always affirmed that Jesus is the Messiah, predicted by the Israelite prophets, and whose coming fulfilled Old Testament divine promises.

Yet, through the multiple layers of my theology, collaged together from thousands of sermons, millions of devotional readings, and the clear declarations of dozens of seminary courses, I had presumed, faithfully, that Jesus was the Messiah, the one who lived out the fulness of God's redemptive purposes proclaimed through Israel. But if I were to set aside all my preconceptions, ignore the many New Testament passages that I had memorized, and step away from my family and church community, with the testimonies and confessions about Jesus that colored the air when I was with them, I wondered whether I could possibly connect Jesus of Nazareth with the prophetic prognostications.

Yes, Jesus was miraculously born. But so were Isaac, Samson, and Samuel.

Yes, people testified that Jesus did miracles. But so did Moses, Joshua, Elijah, and Elisha.

Yes, Jesus self-identified as the "Son of Man," and messenger of God. But so did Ezekiel, Isaiah, Daniel, and a host of other prophets.

Yes, Jesus rose from the dead. But that is also what Jesus' disciples said about Moses and Elijah, who appeared and engaged them on the Mountain of Transfiguration.

What Jesus did not do was end war in our world, cure all diseases, wipe away famine or natural disasters, or bring the nations to judgment for their crimes and rebellions. While human cultures are ever-changing, one would be hard-pressed to say that life on planet earth was significantly different after Jesus showed up than before he came.

Can we say with confidence that Jesus is the Messiah who ushered in the eternal righteous kingdom of God, as foretold by divine revelation through Israel's prophets? The answer to this question is at the heart of Christian theology. The two other great religions that share monotheistic perspectives with Christianity, and also rely on the same prophetic revelation that Christians affirm, each came to different conclusions about Jesus. Jews say that Jesus was certainly a good man, a captivating and dynamic first century rabbi, who did a lot of good and helped many lean into God's ways, rather than ignoring or skirting them. Muslims agree with Jews, and say that Jesus was one of the three greatest prophets ever. In effect, they affirm the perspectives of the good rabbi in my classroom. Jesus is wonderful. We must learn from him. We must listen to him. But the world around us is the strongest testimony that he is neither divine nor the ultimate expression of God's final declarations. Jesus came and taught and healed and prophesied. But the world did not change. The eschaton did not come. The kingdom of God is no nearer now than it was before.

Unless…

Splitting The "Day Of The Lord"
Unless Jesus did something that no one saw coming. Unless Jesus refused to bring in the final expression of the Kingdom of God with a single, mighty THWACK that would have destroyed the bulk of people on earth in the fiery vengeance of God's judgment. Unless Jesus split the "Day of the Lord" in two, initiating its blessings without completing them, absorbing the first blows of divine judgment into himself rather than having the rage of heaven sear like a weapon of destruction across earth, and establishing a remnant troupe of witnesses to change the world for good before Act 2 threatens.

Could it be that the very evidence my rabbi friend put forward to prove that Jesus is not the Messiah, read in another light, might be the testimony that he is precisely the Messiah? Parents know this. They go out for a night, and leave the teens at home. "We will return at 11," they say. "Don't invite others over! No booze! And keep the house relatively neat. Otherwise, you know what's coming!"

They leave. The teens text friends. Social media spreads. A riotous party happens. Neighbors call the police. Destruction reigns and the parents come home to chaos.

They will be true to their words of judgment, to be sure. But the full fury of that righteous punishing will likely be muted, deferred, and partially absorbed in their own losses and pains. They will pay for the cleanup and repairs. They will bail out of jail their children, the ones they love so dearly, even through cries of frustration. They will set new standards, new limits. And that single moment of judgment day will be split and extended into a period of time in which parents act like parents rather than tyrant dictators who unleash the full arsenal in a single quick-reaction doomsday apocalypse.

So it is with the prophetic foretelling of the "Day of the Lord." It is clear from John's identification of Jesus, Jesus' own words to his disciples, and the reflections of the apostles on the meaning of Jesus' coming, that all believed the "Day of the Lord" had arrived in the person of Jesus. Yet, like with Saul the persecutor of Jesus' followers who became Paul the chief witness of Jesus, this mutation of understanding about the Messiah was not easy to comprehend, or immediately apparent.

The Cornerstone Of Christian Theology

Still, this theological shift and new understanding of Jesus' coming is at the heart of Christian testimony. What makes Christianity distinct from Judaism is the belief that the Messiah and the "Day of the Lord" have come in the person of Jesus. What distinguishes Christianity from Islam is the same, along with the proviso that all necessary revelation was culminated in Jesus.

Is Jesus the Messiah, foretold by Israel's prophets? The answer depends on how the Hebrew Bible "Day of the Lord" is understood, and whether Jesus is a failed apocalyptic Jewish rabbi or the genius divine Christ who split the anticipated divine interruption into our history in two, as an act of deep care and blessing for the human race.

Throughout history, people have tried to run ahead of patience by pretending it wasn't needed, that the world would end before they did. The Millerites and the Seventh Day Adventists announced judgment day watches several times over. People climbed trees and sat on roof-tops in all-night vigils. But starry skies never split with angelic celebration and the dreams died with graying dawn. So too did the patience.

A neighboring farmer in my boyhood community was captured by one of these millennial preachers. He sold his farm, bought a motor home, and traveled with his family in caravan with a dozen others chasing the preacher on a whirlwind tour of North America, spreading the news of kingdom come. Six months later they circled the motor homes in Texas and waited — and waited — and waited.

When Jesus refused to do a command curtain call on their schedule, the motor homes began to drift away. The prophetic band broke up, disillusioned with a near-sighted preacher, and our neighbor sneaked back to Minnesota in shame. He died a short while later, tired of patience that gave out before promise.

This is the religious dimension of waiting, watching, and hope that Jesus urged and we find hard to manage. Our world is imperfect, with corners that bump knees and scorpions that poison hands. We get lonely, we get pained; we struggle to survive and are old in body before our youthful ideals get a chance to catch up. We try to find a little comfort and come away addicted to work, booze, drugs, or sex always far short of heaven.

The patience of waiting is tied to our understanding of how time will get resolved into eternity. If there is no God outside the system, we are stuck with cycles of repetition, crushed beneath recurring tasks and tedium that never ends. But if there is a God who has promised to interrupt history with healing and hope and harmony, we wait with expectation.

King Jesus

Someone called Christopher Columbus, the fifteenth-century explorer of North America, the "forerunner of modern government." Why? Well, "Columbus didn't know where he was going when he started; he didn't know where he was when he got there; and he did it all on borrowed money." Does this sound familiar?

Important

Government is always an easy target for criticism. "Being in politics is like being a football coach," said former US Senator Eugene McCarthy. "You have to be smart enough to understand the game and dumb enough to think it's important."

And it *is* important. No society of anarchy has ever survived its own cruelty. Somehow, somewhere, there must be a personification of law and rule and order that holds in check the evil passions of the collective human heart and fosters a sense of purpose and direction and well-being. In one of the most powerful scenes from Robert Bolt's recreation of the life and times of Sir Thomas More, *A Man For All Seasons*, young Roper viewed the corruptness of King Henry VIII's government and said he would cut down every law in England to overthrow him.

But More's energies were fired up, and his words came slicing out: "Oh? And when the last law was down, and the devil turned round on you— where would you hide, Roper, the laws being flat? This country's planted thick with laws from coast to coast . . . and if you cut them down . . . d'you really think you could stand in the winds that would blow?"

Demanding

Pilate was in a quandary as he interviewed Jesus. The strength, the safety, the blessing of the Roman world depends on laws, rules, and allegiance up the chain to the one at the top. The problem with these pesky people of Judea was that they constantly talked about their own king, greater than the emperor in Rome, and worthy alone of devotion.

Then things came to a head in the controversy swirling around this Jewish rabbi from up north. All of Galilee was abuzz about him. When he sauntered into Jerusalem five days ago, the crowds acclaimed him their king. Everything had been in turmoil in that confounded city as Jews from all over the world poured in for this strange "Passover" festival. And in the heightened frenzy of religious devotion and social tensions, the Jewish leaders brought Jesus to Pilate, declaring him seditious. "He claims to be our king!" they told Pilate. "What will the emperor think? What are you going to do about it?"

Jesus seemed so ordinary. How could a simple tradesman command such authority and draw so much attention?

It was not just Pilate who was mystified and confused. For twenty centuries our world has been asking about this captivating man who wielded authority without coercive manipulation.

Mystery

One morning in 1872, David Livingstone wrote this in his diary: "March 19, my birthday. My Jesus, my king, my life, my all, I again dedicate my whole self to thee. Accept me, and grant, O gracious Father, that ere the year is gone I may finish my work. In Jesus' name I ask it. Amen."

Just one year later, servants came to check on their master's delay. They found him on his knees in prayer. He was dead.

Livingstone's testimony was powerful on many levels. But the one that is most striking was his claim upon Jesus as "my king." This has been a common declaration of the church throughout the ages. Even in our era, when democratic social movements topple kings and weigh in against tyrannical regimes, the largest social organization in the entire human race, the church of Jesus Christ, holds as one of its core tenets of belief that Jesus is king.

But why should Jesus be a king? He was born into a poor family during a time of foreign occupation of their country. He was never trained in schools of leadership and had no desire to claim any throne. He seemed to alienate the rich and powerful, rebuffed the efforts of his disciples to start an armed rebellion, hushed the adulation of those who were the recipients of his mighty power, told the existing rulers that if he had a kingdom it was not in direct competition with theirs on their terms, and died an ignoble death meant for the worst of society's scalawags.

Yet from the first connections people made with Jesus, he was often identified as king. Foreigners traveled hundreds of miles to Judea when he was born, telling folks along the way of their astrological readings and projections: a truly great international king had been born! Palestine's powerful King Herod was afraid of Jesus and felt he might be competing for the throne Herod had worked so hard to control. Jesus' own words, while never clearly self-identifying him as a king, were constantly filled with language about the kingdom of heaven or the kingdom of God, of which he seemed to know a great deal more than anyone who was not directly connected with the key governing authority. Then a Roman centurion assigned to Jesus' execution squad, made the remarkable testimony, using language otherwise reserved only for the emperor himself, that "surely *this* man was the Son of God." Somehow people kept viewing Jesus as a king.

The affirmations only continued after Jesus disappeared from the scene. He is above all principalities and powers, Paul wrote, and said that every knee in heaven and on earth would bow to him (Philippians 2). John saw him as an all-powerful ruler (Revelation 1) and had a vision of him as conquering king (19). Even in their prayers, members of the early church addressed Jesus as "sovereign Lord," a term that could hardly be less than royal acknowledgment (Acts 5).

David's Son

How did such nomenclature, which we today take for granted, come about? The key is in the promise made by God through Nathan to David in 2 Samuel 7. David was an unlikely king himself, set on a track to power during Israel's trial run at monarchy under the roller-coaster leadership of King Saul. Although he tried not to compete with the one he knew had also been selected for high office by Yahweh, David increasingly found himself on a trajectory that put him on Israel's throne. Yet he wanted, even there, to affirm that this nation's truest political structure was a theocracy. The God of the Exodus and the Sinai Covenant was Israel's primary ruler.

For this reason David brought the ark of the covenant, Yahweh's portable throne on earth, to Jerusalem, the new capital city of the nation (2 Samuel 6). Moreover, he wished for the building that would house the ark to be a splendid palace, worthy of the nation's great king.

To this task he set his purposes and resources, affirmed, at first, by his advisor, the prophet Nathan (verse 3).

Yet that night Nathan received a new word from the Lord. Although David's desires were laudable, he was too much a man of battle to build a palace of peace. David should gather the resources and make the plans, and then pass along to his son the mandate of temple building.

But the prophetic word went further. Because David had tried to do the right thing, God wanted to honor him in a unique way. Although David was not permitted to build a house for God at this time, God would build a house for David. God made a pledge, a promise, a non-conditioned royal grant covenant to David. For all the years to come, into perpetuity, David would have a descendent on the throne of the nation that was called God's chosen people.

This was an amazing commitment, and it came back in big ways as Israel's history unfolded. Even when Solomon's stupid son Rehoboam should have lost the throne entirely, a remnant of the nation stuck with him as king. Their faithfulness to God's commitments proved accurate, for later the large portion of the nation that split off under Rehoboam's rival Jeroboam was destroyed by the Assyrian empire in 722 BC. Through the shenanigans of Queen Athaliah and King Ahaz, or the turncoat despotism of King Manasseh, or the selfish panderings of Kings Jehoiakin and Zedekiah, Yahweh remained faithful to the divine promise, and the nation survived international threats that beat down many more powerful neighboring kingdoms. In fact, Judah was never really destroyed. While the Assyrians obliterated the northern kingdom, and Judah was made subject to Babylon for a while, a good portion of the nation survived intact as exiles. Eventually they returned to their patrimony and began hoping anew for the return of the Davidic monarchy and national restoration.

That is when good ancestral records became vitally important. Every family connected to the royal line would remember this promise of Yahweh and hope and pray that from their household the next great ruler would arise. So it was, that to an otherwise unimportant couple in Nazareth, about a thousand years after Yahweh made this pledge to David, a miraculous birth happened for two people who were both members of the royal family. On the basis of 2 Samuel 7, Jesus was born a king. While there was much that needed proof and confirmation about his character and his potential, once these things were seen by those around Jesus, the pieces quickly fell into place. That is why, when Jesus entered Jerusalem a week before his crucifixion, the crowds could shout with certainty and conviction, "Hosanna to the Son of David!" King Jesus had arrived.

Gift

For Israel, through the centuries of her sometimes much scarred existence, the promise of an eternal reign for David's great sons was like Christmas gifts bought early in November or December, and packaged prettily for display under a tree until Christmas. One even has my name on it; all in the family know that it will bring me wonder and joy and blessing, but its exact content remains a mystery until the wrappings are ripped away. So too with God's long-planned activity of salvation. The package was clearly set before the world in the national identity of Israel; but until the specifics of the gift were revealed through the person of Jesus, it remained a "mystery." Even the prophets were somewhat in the dark about the exact contours of the great gift that was to be revealed. But the wrappings were off, and the proclamation of Jesus was the hope of the world, even if it completely confused Pilate.

Some gifts we receive are simply add-ons to the polite niceties of the relationship. For instance, a man might give a woman a book as a Christmas gift. He knows she likes to read, and this happens to be a best-seller she has not yet gotten into, so he gives it to her as a reflection of his thoughtfulness.

At a second level, however, other gifts might more directly tie into their relationship. He might buy a bottle of expensive perfume. When she opens the gift, she is not only aware of his care, but also enters a conspiracy with him toward a deepening level for their friendship. She applies the perfume to her body, and its scent becomes part of their special language of love. When she uses the perfume, she thinks uniquely of him. When he smells the perfume, he thinks solely of her. The gift is not simply an add-on in their friendship; it has become a symbol of their relationship itself.

But there is also a third level of gifting. Suppose the man and the woman are married. Along with gifts like books and perfumes, they also have sexual intercourse as an expression of their love. When a baby is born, it is a gift for both of them, since neither could produce it alone. Yet it is more than just an outside gift that is brought into the relationship; it is itself the relationship come to expression. The gift is not just a thoughtful gesture (level 1) or even a meaningful enhancement to the relationship (level 2); this gift is the essence of the relationship come alive in a unique and special way (level 3).

So it is with Jesus. In the past, God spoke of the divine commitment of care to the human race (providence; level 1). God also gave unique testimony of love through the nation of Israel (revelation; level 2). God comes to live with us, to be part of our world, and to transform our lives in ways that we had never before considered (salvation; level 3).

Pilate did not know what he was dealing with that confusing day in Jerusalem. But God knew — and we know. And because of King Jesus, everything has changed.

Japanese evangelist Toyohiko Kagawa told of the fears that were part of the world he grew up in. He spoke of the day that he first understood the message of the gospel. He put it this way: "The good tidings of Jesus lie in the belief that the essence of the universe is an affectionate creator, however dark the night may be and however fiercely the tempest may roar."

Let the "Pomp and Circumstance" marches roll!

www.ingramcontent.com/pod-product-compliance
Lightning Source LLC
Chambersburg PA
CBHW022028090426
42739CB00006BA/338